FERMFOLK
AND
FISHERFOLK

FERMFOLK
— & —
FISHERFOLK

**Rural Life in Northern Scotland in the Eighteenth
and Nineteenth Centuries**

edited by
JOHN S. SMITH and DAVID STEVENSON

ABERDEEN UNIVERSITY PRESS

First published 1989
Aberdeen University Press
A member of the Maxwell Pergamon Macmillan Group

© The contributors 1989

British Library Cataloguing in Publication Data
Fermfolk and fisherfolk: rural life in Northern
   Scotland in the eighteenth and nineteenth centuries.
   1. Scotland. Rural regions. Social conditions, history
I. Smith, S. J. (John Smart) II. Stevenson, David,
   1942–
   941.1′009′734

ISBN 0 08 037733 5

Typeset from author-generated discs
and printed by AUP Glasgow/Aberdeen—A member of BPCC Ltd.

CONTENTS

ILLUSTRATIONS

PREFACE

This is the fourth collection of papers to be published based on the local history day conferences organised by the Centre for Scottish Studies and the Department of Adult Education and Extra-Mural Studies of the University of Aberdeen. The conference, held on 29 October 1988, was gratifying both through the continuing local support for these occasions reflected in the size of the audience, and through the stimulating quality of the papers presented. The fact that I myself had to deliver one of the papers through the illness of its author may have meant that its full value was not evident, which makes it doubly useful to have it available in print.

Thanks are due to the authors of the papers for allowing them to be published; to Rod Gunson, the Centre's Conference organiser, and staff of the Department of Adult Education, for their hard work behind the scenes; and to the chairmen of the morning and afternoon sessions of the conference, Jim Buchan (Rector of Peterhead Academy) and Andrew Hill (Curator of the North East Scotland Agricultural Heritage Centre, Aden Country Park, Mintlaw).

DAVID STEVENSON
Director of the Centre for Scottish Studies
and Reader in Scottish History
University of Aberdeen

THE BACKGROUND TO PLANNED VILLAGE FOUNDATION IN NORTH EAST SCOTLAND

John S. Smith

All rural settlement patterns in long settled areas are a mixture of the old and the new, forming a palimpsest of nuclei—each the product of a particular phase in the historical and technological development of the countryside. In North East Scotland the most formative in a series of surges of landscape change took place in the period from 1750 to 1830. The results are written large on the contemporary rural landscape. Within a period of eighty years most of the farming townships which appear on Roy's Map of 1749 and which had been the foci of agricultural endeavour for centuries were broken up into single farmsteads dispersed amongst the newly enclosed fields. Previously unsettled areas were infilled with crofts, biting into the fringes of mosses and commonties, while attempts were made to reclaim even exceptionally stony ground. The old names of the townships persisted in the new individualised units but qualified by prefixes such as Mid, Nether, Upper and Lower.

Over the same period, a new breed of villages began to spring up augmenting, and eventually superceding an old established pattern of hamlets whose historical *raisons d'être* were clearly indicated by their names of kirktoun and milltoun. Long established market villages like Insch, Clatt and Daviot maintained their weekly and annual markets, although hamlet and village alike were eventually to be overshadowed in size and function by the new planned villages, many distinguished by the prefix 'New'. The inland planned villages considered in this essay, like

1

their coastal counterparts, were the result of an individual's decision to innovate within the framework of estate boundaries, rather than forming part of a coherent regional strategy. Thus landowners were the initiators of rural development strategies over the period within which the planned villages played an important role. The coastal fishing villages (which are considered in a separate chapter) were socially and physically divorced from the countryside, forming in the words of the Whitehills parish minister 'a society quite distinct—not just in surname, but differing from those inland by their fair clear complexions, and by the superior comeliness of the females'.[1] Strichen, Lumsden, New Pitsligo, Tomintoul and New Deer are examples of the new inland planned village foundations, most of whom were closely associated with estate improvements.

Village foundation was favoured by a natural increase in the rural population and by the ongoing structural changes in farming, both of which created a surplus population in the countryside. The landlord response of village foundation would in modern terminology be termed the creation of a number of *points d'appui*, even growth points, where a measure of point investment through subsidisation of feuars could in theory increase estate revenue through the ultimately increased rentals derived from development of rural industries performed in the home. In a few cases, the motivations to be found may have been more esoteric. Sir John Sinclair, the Caithness improver noted that 'it is from the temperate and healthy families of the country labourer and tradesmen and not from the alleys and garrets of the town, that the race is to be sought who are best calculated to cultivate our fields or to defend our properties from danger—villagers are in general contented and unambitious'.[2] In the aftermath of the 'internal war' (the '45 Jacobite Rising), the Inspectors of Forfeited Estates avowed that 'nothing was more likely to civilise the inhabitants of upland Aberdeenshire and Banffshire than the plantation of villages, all with linenworks, post-offices, market and prison', adding rather cynically that such promotions might convert the Highland people 'from their idle and wicked practices to commerce and trade'.[3] The urge to promote rural industry is confirmed by Lord Strichen who, in his own words, founded the village which bears his name for 'the promotion of the Arts and Manufacturers of this country, and for the accommodation of tradesmen of all denominations, manufacturers and other industrious people to settle'.[4]

It is clear from these opinions and statements of intent that there were varying motivations behind inland village foundations, and that they were not simply designed for the resettlement of a local population displaced by agricultural improvements. Indeed, in several cases, there was a measure of selection involved in letting feus. In the case of Tomintoul, potential settlers had to find a local person of standing to attest that they were 'very honest, harmless men'.[5]

Once the decision had been taken to found, how was the site chosen? Sir John Sinclair's criteria for site selection, written in the 1830s, at least confirms the appropriateness of his nickname of 'Agricultural Sir John'. 'The situation ought to be well sheltered and rather elevated for purity of air and in the neighbourhood of a stream or at any rate well supplied with good water. Although the labour and manure which the village furnishes will, in good time, fertilise any land, yet if possible, the soil in its neighbourhood should be naturally well suited for garden culture.'[6]

The location of the village was a compromise between existing communication systems and the estate boundaries of the founder. A 'centrical' position within the duke of Gordon's estates was claimed for Tomintoul, while New Pitsligo lay on a merchants' route. For Grantown on Spey, newspaper advertisements detailed its location as being 'near to Speybridge, has public roads branching off from it to Inverness, Nairn, Forres, Elgin, Keith, Braemar and Perth, and to the West Highlands, being eighteen miles from Inverness and twelve from Forres'.[7] The final site, chosen after a careful survey carried out by Peter May of Aberdeen, was by no means prepossessing. It was 'a barren heath moor barely capable of providing grazing for a score of sheep'.[8] Equally typical sites were on moorland edges, low plateaux and even on the side of small hills, each offering the important assets of easily available building stone and peat fuel. Where handloom weaving was envisaged as a significant factor in village growth, water power and potential sites for bleaching and retting were siting constraints. There does not seem to be any direct evidence for choosing sites to minimise the loss of quality agricultural land. Once a site was chosen and

1. New Pitsligo, built on the side of a hill, between a source of building stone at the top, and a source of peat at the bottom.

surveyed, plots were usually marked out on the ground and a set of local regulations drawn up, with areas for stone quarrying and peat extraction identified.

The new villages were promoted by newspaper advertising, especially when they were not designed specifically as part of the internal reorganisation of an estate. The *Aberdeen Journal* advertisements for Grantown in April 1765 describe 'the place proposed for the town as a good pleasant country, and well accommodated with all materials for building, lies near plenty moss and other firing, has the Woods of Abernethy near it, and a fine limestone quarry easily wrought'.[9] Grantown was designed to replace Castleton of Freuchie, a local marketing centre situated about half a mile south west of Castle Grant. The new laird, James Grant of Grant, appears to have been extremely keen to improve his Strathspey estates and employed surveyor Alexander Taylor to make a careful survey of the

2. The linear form of the street village is classically displayed by Lumsden, Aberdeenshire. Such simple planned village layouts involved a minimum of planning effort. (Gordon Stables, Department of Geography, University of Aberdeen)

proposed site. His plan reveals a regular layout with central square and single long road. The first fifty feus are plotted. Each of the original settlers was assigned equal portions of ground, all with access to supplies of peat and to a large enclosure of land assigned as common grazing ground. The leases were for ninety-nine years.

The street village with central square and variants on a grid layout of feus was a fairly standard design, combining simplicity with maximisation of plot density.[10] Lanes running at right angles to the main street in many planned villages provided access for wheeled transport to the fields and peat mosses. There is a habitual absence of front gardens, with the houses set directly on the main street, presumably to avoid the usage of such areas for the accumulation of household rubbish. Behind the houses ran the long rectangular plots with space for work-shops, kaleyard and a cow. The specific building regulations varied according to the landowners' taste. At Strichen and at New Leeds—both on Lord Strichen's estate—two stone chimneys on each house was an essential requirement! The major public buildings were usually provided by the landowner—the church and inn, for example, and the size of the former gives a clear indication of his aspirations for the future growth of the village population.

A few planned villages were designed with improved amenity in mind. Before the present settlement of Fochabers in Moray was laid out, the old hamlet sat within the policies of Gordon Castle. In 1776, the Eton-educated duke of Gordon ordered his factor to 'bargain for and purchase from the feuars the present village of Fochabers'.[11] It is not clear whether the duke had heard of the then fashionable vogue of isolating the mansion from the village, or whether the re-siting arose out of the stealing of the castle washing of which the duchess complained, but in any case, architects employed to improve the castle and its grounds were also given the task of submitting plans for the new village. The plan finally adopted took the form of a central square bisected by an axial street, with the southern side of the square reserved for the parish church.

Even in Grantown, the decision to found may have been not unrelated to the nearness of the castleton to Castle Grant. In this case, James Grant envisaged the village as the high point in a wider package of estate improvements which were initiated in 1763. These included tree-planting, agricultural im-provements, road building and incentives to encourage people to settle in his Strathspey estates. Free rentals for up to seven years were on offer especially for 'reduced private soldiers' taking up any quantity of land from five to fifteen acres with a view to improving. Credit and money loans were also available in the campaign to attract settlers. A number of industrial concerns were financed by the estate, while all fairs and markets within the estate were centralised in Grantown. Grantown's building regulations instructed those taking a feu 'to build regular and fronting the street with stone and lime walls, and to cover the roofs with slate, and to build dykes round the gardens, to keep houses in proper and decent repair'.[12] It was also noted that all residents must keep their peats, turf, fire and dunghills in their back courts and allow 'nothing of that kind to be or remain at the front of their houses—under penalty of five shillings fine'. The first leasee was John Grant, a weaver from Rothiemichael who began construction of a 'manufactory house' designed to accommodate six looms in 1765. By 1768, sixteen feus had been taken up, with a total of twenty buildings erected. Feuholders included two manufacturers, a weaver, a tailor, a vintner, a mason and a shoemaker, but the relatively slow progress encouraged the laird to run a second series of advertisements in 1768 stating that 'very convenient and advantageous units remain'.[13] Grant brought in Thomas Cornish, a stocking manufacturer from England, and provided him with financial assistance to the tune of £1,200 plus accommodation. The Cornish stocking enterprise was eventually to employ forty-two men and women. By 1794, the earl of Fife in a letter to Lady Grant felt justified in describing Grantown as an 'industrious city'.[14] By then in addition to the tradesmen, Grantown had twelve merchants keeping shops, two schools, a brewery and three public houses. However, by 1807 only four weavers were cited in Grantown's feuholders list, implying that isolation from wool sources and markets together with the growth of major industrial producers of woollen goods like Aberdeen were seriously undermining Grantown's original *raison d'être*. Other planned villages performed better in the first few decades of the nineteenth century. Writing of New Pitsligo in 1840, the parish minister noted that 'its two main streets are linked with rows of neatly built houses, one street fully a mile in length'.[15] Of the population of 1,200 resident in 1840, around ninety were employed in the domestic manufacture of cotton and linen cloth, the remainder in agricultural labouring or cultivating their small plots of land. By 1864, with a population of just under 2,000, New Pitsligo could claim to be the largest village in Scotland. The village occupied the ground formerly utilised by a mere three fermtouns. The parish minister ventured to suggest that the major selling points in its successful growth in population had been inexhaustible supplies of moss and an abundance of reclaimable land available from the proprietor on nineteen year leases. The strategy of a mixed village economy—both between and within occupations—appears to have been

particularly typical in Buchan. The 1772 newspaper advertisements for New Byth (founded nine years previous), while
seeking industrious weavers, nonetheless notes that 'married
men who have families can be accommodated with a croft of
land, and cows, grass and fire, at an easy rate'.

As befits villages founded by personal initiative, although
there are similarities in groundplan, site characteristics and
general *raison d'être*'s, each has its individual story. Each was
founded with great expectations after careful survey work. In
1775 surveyor George Milne produced a 'plan for a village at
Tomintoul'. The cost for eight days survey and five days drawing out a fair copy was £4. 9s. 0d. It was then envisaged as 'a
very proper place for a bleachfield and spinning school' with
'this most centrical place' designed to 'soon become the most
populous place in the country'.[16] Despite advertising in 1776,
by 1791 only eight feus were taken up, and three years later,
the *Statistical Account* noted that Tomintoul was 'inhabited by
thirty-seven families with not a single manufacture to employ
them'. The minister went on to stress 'that all of them sell
whisky and all of them drink it. When disengaged from this
business, the women spin yarns, kiss their inamoratas, or dance
to the discordant strains of an old fiddle'.[17] Despite the reference
to the spinning of yarn, one tends to suspect that the illicit
distillation of whisky provided the mainstay of the local economy in the 1790s—not quite what the duke of Gordon had in
mind for his planned village. Writing in her Journal for 6
September 1860, Queen Victoria described Tomintoul as 'the
most tumbledown, poor looking place I ever saw—a long street
with three inns and miserable, dirty looking houses and people
with a sad look of wretchedness about them'.[18]

By 1850, around four hundred and fifty planned villages had
been founded with varying degrees of initial success.[19] With
their characteristic regular layout, these capital projects
initiated by landowners loom large on the landscape of Lowland
Scotland. Many display little evidence of visible support in
terms of employment structure. Their atmosphere to the passing
traveller recalls the memorable phrase of John R. Allan who
immortalised Aberchirder (Foggieloan) as a 'place where folk
practise all the ancient virtues and some of the ancient vices,
while waiting for something to happen'.[20] Nonetheless, despite

3. A central square as at Rhynie, Aberdeenshire, incorporated within a grid plan, is again pleasingly simple, but offers the facility of a central open space for market and amenity. (Gordon Stables, Department of Geography, University of Aberdeen)

varying *floruit* in span and range of initial intended economy, these inland planned villages remain the most common village type in the countryside of North East Scotland, creating a range of problems for the contemporary rural planning scene which their originators would not have forseen.

REFERENCES

1. *New Statistical Account of Scotland* (Edinburgh, 1845), 13, 220.
2. Sir John Sinclair, *Analysis of the Statistical Account of Scotland* (Edinburgh, 1831), 177 *et seq.*
3. A.H. Millar (ed), *Scottish Forfeited Estates Papers, 1715-1745* (Scottish History Society, Edinburgh, 1909), 159.

4. 'History of Strichen', *Transactions of the Buchan Field Club*, 2 (1891-2), 68.
5. V. Gaffney, *The Lordship of Strathavon— Tomintoul under the Gordons* (Third Spalding Club, Aberdeen, 1960), 58.
6. Sinclair, *Analysis*, 177 *et seq.*
7. *Aberdeen Journal*, 15 April 1765 (advertisement).
8. Scottish Record Office [SRO], Seafield Papers, GD 248/25/2/6, Notes on the scheme propos'd for erecting the village of Grantstown. Cited in D.G. Lockhart, 'The planned villages' in M.L. Parry and T.R. Slater (eds.), *The making of the Scottish countryside*, (London, 1980), 255.
9. *Aberdeen Journal*, 15 April 1765.
10. D.G. Lockhart, 'Scottish village plans, a preliminary analysis, *Scottish Geographical Magazine*, 96 (1980), 141-57.
11. Charles McKean, *The district of Moray—an illustrated architectural guide* (Edinburgh, 1987), 116.
12. SRO, GD 248, Box 25, Bundle 2, Castle Grant Papers, Regulations for the Village of Grantown.
13. *Aberdeen Journal*, 15 June 1768 (advertisement).
14. Sir W. Fraser, *The chiefs of Grant* (3 vols., Edinburgh, 1883), ii, 484 (Letter from 2nd earl of Fife to Lady Grant, 17 August 1784).
15. *New Statistical Account of Scotland* (Edinburgh, 1845), xii, 725.
16. Gaffney, *Landship of Strathavon*.
17. Sir John Sinclair (ed.), *Statistical Account of Scotland* (Edinburgh, 1794), xii, 439-40.
18. Queen Victoria, *Leaves from the journal of our life in the Highlands from 1848 to 1861* (London, 1868), 199.
19. D.G. Lockhart, 'Migration to planned villages in Scotland between 1725 and 1850', *Scottish Geographical Magazine* , 102 (1986), 165.
20. J.R. Allan, *North-East Lowlands of Scotland* (London, 1952), 21.

MIGRATION TO PLANNED VILLAGES IN NORTH EAST SCOTLAND

Douglas G. Lockhart

Planned villages founded by landowners during the eighteenth and nineteenth century are a common occurrence throughout the Scottish countryside and the North East can boast more than seventy examples. The straight roads, squares and rectangular building plots so characteristic of these settlements are testimony to careful planning by their founders, and several have been recognised as worthy of conservation status. There are many reasons for the construction of such a dense network of villages. Most were associated with agricultural improvement and the rationalisation of holdings, but many had additional functions such as markets and fairs, together with a limited amount of textile manufacturing. The villages offered a refuge for displaced agricultural labour and cottars who could rent fields, known as lotted lands, and pursue part-time farming. This kind of work supplemented earnings from labouring and rural crafts.

Landowners were also keen to develop industry even if it meant providing loans and subsidies to entrepreneurs. In the more remote areas, lairds felt that a thriving textile industry was essential to a community's well-being. Sir James Grant, founder of Grantown-on-Spey, spent more than £3,000 on assisting manufacturers during the first twenty-five years of its existence. Also in Speyside, the earliest settlers of Archiestown were the linen manufacturer and his workforce of weavers on whom much hope for the future success of the village lay.

On the coast, a series of settlements were built, some in conjunction with major harbour works (Burghead, Branderburgh) while others had more modest quays (Boddam, Sand-haven). Fishermen, tradesmen such as coopers and curers, as well as ubiquitous craftsmen were attracted. In short, planned villages housed heterogeneous populations engaged in a wide range of occupations. They were attracted by security of tenure, home-ownership, employment opportunities and occasionally financial inducements.

Landowners viewed planned villages with a mixture of pride and economic pragmatism. Certainly, several of the better known places such as Fochabers and the New Town of Cullen were designed to enhance the appearance of the estate but, most were dominated by uniform rows of cottages with only a few two-storey houses and a church to provide some variety. These communities received their share of criticism from early tourists like Henry Skrine, a native of Warley in Somerset, who noted that New Byth was 'famous for nothing but the wretchedness of its accommodation' and Robert Southey, the poet-laureate who lamented at the utopian sameness of the cottages in Rothes. Nevertheless, these and many other villages brought very sub-stantial gains to estate income from feu-duties and field rents and early village planners quickly grasped the simple economics of village founding. Money laid out in physical planning and subsidies was quickly recouped from a growing rental. In this respect, Sir Archibald Grant, founder of Archiestown and adviser to Joseph Cumine during the planning of Cuminestown, had a very clear point to make: 'the proposed village is the... only mean to Improve land with Expence and with certain profit...'

Although many planned villages remained small, with popu-lations under five hundred, there are few examples of total failure. The study of migration patterns is perhaps one of the most fundamental issues in the history of Scotland's planned villages. Certainly quite large numbers of families must have been involved, however, the task of reconstructing this move-ment of population is fraught with difficulties due to the frag-mented nature of the source material.

Sources. A general impression of the movement of settlers can be gleaned from the parish descriptions in the *Statistical Account* published in the 1790s and the *New Statistical Account*, which

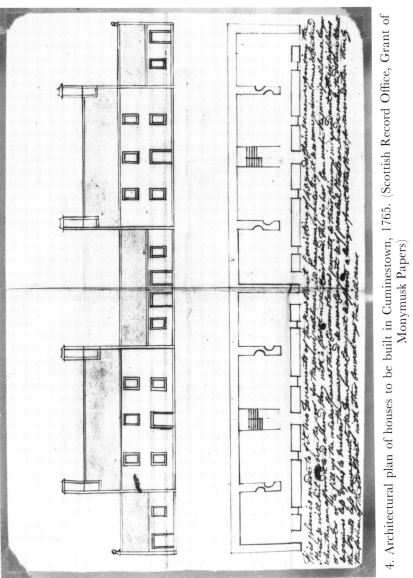

4. Architectural plan of houses to be built in Cuminestown, 1765. (Scottish Record Office, Grant of Monymusk Papers)

appeared in the 1840s. These fall short on detail and it is necessary to examine a wide range of legal sources: feu-charters and long leases, the former preserved in the Particular Register of Sasines in the Scottish Record Office in Edinburgh; chartulary books held by solicitors, and estate papers some of which are in Aberdeen University Library while others relating to the North East are in Edinburgh repositories. These provide information on the occupation and former place of residence of migrants. In addition, estate papers (correspondence, plans, rentals and memoranda) give a detailed insight into how villages were planned, tradesmen were persuaded to settle and sometimes background information on individual families as well. The files of local newspapers are also worth searching for landowners' advertisements which describe the site and feuing terms and give an address to obtain further information.

The records for fishing villages are thinner because of the practice of issuing short leases (tenancy-at-will or seven years) to fishermen. Many of these agreements have been lost with the passage of time. However, from the beginning of the nineteenth century, the depth of source material gradually improves and by mid-century, census data and trades directories provide comprehensive information on birth-place, family structure and employment.

Migration patterns. The process of planning villages followed a very similar sequence in most cases, and this is true not just of the North East but among the four hundred and fifty planned villages throughout Scotland. The first stage involved taking the decision to build a village, though in practice this was often a matter of following a neighbouring landowner's plan of action. There are many examples of this trend: New Keith and Newmill; Cuminestown and New Byth are typical, but the network of friendship among landowners stretched throughout the length and breadth of the region and exchanges of views and planning documents was very common. Some landowners even built second and third villages on their estates and Cummingston, Dallas and Covesea, all on Sir William Gordon Cumming's lands in Morayshire, are not unique. The next step involved selecting the site. This was dependent on a number of factors, principally the existing road network, availability of

5. The classic grid iron layout of Ballater was developed on a barren *muir* as part of a package of estate improvements which included promotion of mineral springs, devised by returned Jacobite Farquharson of Monaltrie. (Jim Livingston, Department of Geography, University of Aberdeen)

land out of lease to be granted as lotted lands, peat moss for fuel and adequate water supplies. Land of indifferent quality was often chosen because this could be improved by intensive draining and manuring and offered the greatest potential for medium-term increases in rent levels. These criteria also applied to fishing villages and in addition it was crucial to locate the settlement close to a suitable creek or point on the coast where a harbour could be built. While it is true to say that many of the older seatowns lacked formal harbour facilities, planned fishing villages to be successful needed to woo fishermen away

TABLE 1

Average migration distances by type of planned village (km)

Village	Type	average distance	maximum distance
Archiestown	tradesman-agricultural	21.5	55.0
Auchenblae	tradesman-agricultural	9.5	38.5
Carnoustie[1]	tradesman-suburban	4.0	19.0
Friockheim	tradesman-agricultural	10.0	37.0
Gardenstown	maritime	9.5	67.0
Hopeman	maritime	12.5	56.0
Strichen	tradesman-agricultural	15.0	32.0

1. Data were collected for three planned villages in the vicinity of Carnoustie: Gardynebourg, Hunter's Town and Newton of Panbride.

from these older settlements and for this reason most had harbours. The few new villages which were inconveniently located in relation to creeks (Cummingston; Rattray) remained small-scale.

Once the site had been chosen, a landsurveyor was appointed to draw up a plan and peg out the village site. In some places it is possible to establish many of the details of the survey. For Fife Keith, founded in 1817, even the surveyor's accounts for lodging and meals taken at a local inn have survived! All that remained to do was to attract settlers. Some villages, such as Fochabers and the New Town of Cullen, were built specifically to re-house the population of old settlements that were about to be cleared, and therefore inherited an existing community structure. Others were built to coincide with major land reorganisation, for instance Strichen, Dallas and Dufftown, and are likely to have acquired some tradesmen and labourers already resident on the estate. However, the peopling of the majority of villages in the North East was only achieved after advertising. The most common method was the newspaper advertisement, and dozens of examples can be found in the files of the *Aberdeen Journal* and the *Inverness Journal*. Usually notices were placed in the local newspaper indicating an expectation to

6. Balvenie Street, Dufftown. (George Washington Wilson Collection, University of Aberdeen)

New Village upon the Estate of the Right Honourable James Earl of Fife near Keith, to be disegnated or named FIFE-KEITH,

THE plan of the Village comprehends 165 Lots to be given off and held in Feu Farm. But it is intended to dispose of only about one half of that number at present.

EACH feu contains 25 falls of ground, except where otherways mentioned in the following List—and in general the extent of front is 45 feet, besides an opening of 10 feet between each couple of feus as shown upon the plan.

THE Feu Duty annexed to each is to be payable at Whitsunday yearly. It is proposed to give possession immediately, but no Feu Duty to be exacted until Whitsunday 1818. Any entry money that may be agreed upon, shall be paid at the time of getting access.

No.	BRIDGE STREET.	Feu Duty.	No.		Feu Duty.	No.		Feu Duty.
1	Of Plan 40 falls of ground,	£. 1 - 10 -	26	. . . . .	£. 1 - 0 -	72	. . . . .	£. 1 - 5 -
2	. . . . .	1 - 0 -	27	. . . .	1 - 0 -	73	. . . .	1 - 5 -
3	. . . . .	1 - 0 -	28	. . . .	1 - 0 -	74	. . . .	1 - 5 -
4	. . . . .	1 - 0 -	29	Double Feu, or 50 Falls,	2 - 0 -	75	. . . .	1 - 5 -
5	. . . . .	1 - 0 -	30	. . . .	1 - 0 -	76	Corner Feu,	1 - 10 -
6	. . . . .	1 - 0 -	31	. . . .	1 - 0 -			
	WELLINGTON TERRACE.		32	. . . .	1 - 0 -		FIFE STREET.	
			33	. . . .	1 - 0 -			
			34	. . . .	1 - 0 -	77	Corner Feu,	1 - 10 -
7	. . . .	1 - 5 -	35	. . . .	1 - 0 -	78	. . . .	1 - 5 -
8	. . . .	1 - 5 -	36	. . . .	1 - 0 -	79	. . . .	1 - 5 -
9	. . . .	1 - 5 -	54	35 Falls, .	1 - 10 -	80	. . . .	1 - 5 -
10	. . . .	1 - 5 -	55	. . . .	1 - 0 -	81	. . . .	1 - 5 -
11	. . . .	1 - 5 -	56	. . . .	1 - 0 -	82	. . . .	1 - 5 -
12	. . . .	1 - 5 -	57	17 Falls, -	1 - 0 -	83	. . . .	1 - 5 -
13	. . . .	1 - 5 -	58	- " " "	1 - 0 -	84	. . . .	1 - 5 -
14	. . . .	1 - 5 -	61	- " " "	1 - 0 -	85	. . . .	1 - 5 -
15	. . . .	1 - 5 -	62	- " " "	1 - 0 -	60	Corner, - -	1 - 10 -
16	. . . .	1 - 5 -	63	29 Falls, -	1 - 10 -	59	Corner, - -	1 - 10 -
17	. . . .	1 - 5 -	64	- " " "	1 - 10 -	86	- " " "	1 - 5 -
18	. . . .	1 - 5 -	65	- " " "	1 - 5 -	87	- " " "	1 - 5 -
19	. . . .	1 - 5 -	66	- " " "	1 - 5 -	88	- " " "	1 - 5 -
20	. . . .	1 - 5 -	67	Siutrell Croft House to be possessed by Mrs. Lawson.		89	- " " "	1 - 5 -
21	. . . .	1 - 5 -				90	- " " "	1 - 5 -
	REGENT STREET.			NELSON TERRACE.		91	- " " "	1 - 5 -
						92	. . . .	1 - 5 -
22	Thirty Eight falls, .	1 - 10 -	68	. . . .	1 - 5 -	93	. . . .	1 - 5 -
23	. . . .	1 - 0 -	69	- " " "	1 - 5 -	64	Corner, . .	1 - 10 -
24	. . . .	1 - 0 -	70	- " " "	1 - 5 -	104	Coopethill, Suanybrae say 40 falls,	1 - 10 -
25	. . . .	1 - 0 -	71	- " " "	1 - 5 -			£. 93 - 15 -
							In all 77 feus besides Siutrell Croft House.	

7. Handbill promoting Fife Keith, 1817. (Fife Mss M series bundle LXVI K 43. By kind permission of Captain Alexander Ramsay of Mar)

recruit settlers from the immediate area. Handbills, sometimes reprints of the press notice were also pinned to market crosses, inns and church doors. More active forms of recruitment were occasionally pursued. Invitations to attend meetings on the village site (New Aberdour) or at an inn nearby (New Leeds) where refreshments were provided enabled prospective settlers to view the site and discuss terms with the landowner and his factor. In new fishing villages, estate management would visit neighbouring communities in an attempt to persuade fishermen to sign contracts. The account book for Portgordon shows that twelve shillings was spent on whisky at the signing ceremony, and when Cummingston was being founded there was an amusing excursion by Sir William Gordon Cumming's factor and a baillie from Nairn who travelled to Avoch in the Black Isle in a vain effort to recruit local fishermen. Having failed there, they turned their attention to Portessie, only to be accused of poaching drunken fishermen attending a wedding. What all this evidence points to is the inescapable conclusion that recruitment efforts were concentrated in the local area and that migration would largely be characterised by short-distance moves.

The data in estate and legal sources supports this impression. Average migration distances are invariably short, just 9km to Auchenblae and Gardenstown for example. Only on the highland margins were average distances somewhat greater: for Archiestown the mean rises to 21.5km. As more villages were built, so it became unnecessary to migrate more than 20km to reach a new village. A wide range of occupations were present, however employment was dominated by rural crafts, textiles and agriculture and a typical picture of occupational structure is that of Rothes towards the close of the eighteenth century (Table 3).

A LL *Manufacturers, Mechanicks and Merchants who incline to take Feus, or long Tacks, at the Market Muir of Strichen, may apply to Peter Thomson at Strichen-house, or James Adamson at the Bridge, who will inform them of the Conditions. There is plenty of Stone, Lime, and inexhaustible Moss, a weekly Market, and four great Fairs annually : the Situation is within six Miles of nine Fish-towns, and would be a most convenient Receptacle for all Persons concerned in the Linnen Manufacturies, as there is plenty of Yarn already spun in the Country, and a Flax mill to be erected at the intended Village.*

8. Newspaper advertisement for Strichen, Aberdeenshire. (*Aberdeen Journal*, 21 November 1763)

TABLE 2
Migration to Archiestown between 1761 and 1772

Place of origin and National Grid reference	Names	Employment	Distance (km)
Anagach (NJ 037267)	William Stewart	carpenter	30
Auchvochkie (NJ 146351)	William Stuart	squarewright	13
Balvenie (NJ 321424)	James Thomson	mason/squarewright	9
Boattown of Wester Elchies (NJ 260428)	George Gray	boatman	3
Buchromb (NJ 312437)	Andrew Anderson	taylor	8.5
Cairns of Ballintomb (NJ 247445)	James McRobert	—	1.5
Carron (NJ 237413)	John and James Thompson	merchant	2.5
Corglass (NJ 153418)	John and James McDonald	square and wheelwright masons and dykers	8
Cullen	Thomas Anderson	weaver/manufacturer	44
Drumfurrich (NJ 293442)	Hugh Cameron	weaver	6
Easter Galdwell (NJ 321456)	Robert Fleming	—	8
Elgin	Lachlan Dunbar	manufacturer	23
Fochabers	James Hay	weaver	17.5
Huntly	Charles, John and Alex Laing	weavers	37
Keith	Jo Brebner		30
	John Ogg	lintdresser	
Knockdow of Ballintomb (NJ 215425)	John Lee	gardener	2
Laggan of Ballintomb (NJ 235417)	Donald Cruickshank	—	2
Loanend (NJ 489353)	John Wear	mason	40
Macallan (NJ 275444)	Alex Stuart	wheelwright	5
Newtown (NJ 162637)	John and James Thomson	taylors	26
Portsoy	Alex Kerr	linen weaver	52
	William Anderson	mason	
Taminachty (NJ 300460)	John McKonnachy	mason	7
Tullochallum (NJ 341393)	James Mackie	mason	13
Wester Elchies (NJ 255430)	John McRobert	cooper	3
	John and William Hay	—	

Source: SRO, Grant of Monymusk Papers GD 345/1014.

TABLE 3

Occupations of tenants of lotted lands at Rothes, Morayshire, 1798

Occupational group	%
agriculture	7.1
crafts	66.1
textiles	17.9
shops and inns	5.4
merchants	1.8
professional	1.8

Note: There were 56 tenants whose occupation was stated: a further 22 occupations were not stated.
Sources:
SRO, Seafield Papers, GD 248/2258, Rental of the Moray Collection Crop 1798.

Longer distance migrants were usually people with special skills, such as the three Laing brothers (all weavers) who moved from Huntly to Archiestown to begin work in the linen factory, or capitalists such as manufacturers and merchants attracted by prospects of financial inducements and a period of profitable trading. Many had urban origins, such as Stuartfield's first bleacher who also originated in Huntly, and the manager of the linen factory in Archiestown who came from Cullen.

Most households moved singly and there is only limited evidence that chain migration took place, that is one migration leading to another. Actual statements that two migrants were related are comparatively rare so common surnames and other indicators such as purchase of adjacent building plots by persons with the same surname and joint purchase of plots were used in an attempt to estimate the extent of linked migration. Such migration varied considerably, in some places fewer than 5 per cent of household heads may have been related while in others the proportion exceeded 40 per cent. Nor surprisingly at the lower level were the smallest villages while the highest values were recorded in fishing communities where boat crews migrated together as one unit. As a rule, fishermen tended to migrate longer distances than tradesmen and often they lived

9. High Street, Strichen. (George Washington Wilson Collection, University of Aberdeen)

TABLE 4

Birth place of male household heads in selected planned villages in Buchan, 1851 (%)

Villages	same parish	other Buchan parishes	other Aberdeenshire	adjacent counties	other Scottish counties	England/ Wales/ Ireland	unknown/ illegible	number of household heads
Burnhaven	3.8	88.5	3.8	—	—	—	3.8	26
Fetterangus	32.1	50.0	10.7	3.6	1.8	—	1.8	56
Garmond	40.5	18.9	21.6	—	8.1	2.7	8.1	37
Mintlaw	25.4	61.0	3.4	5.1	5.1	—	—	59
New Aberdour	44.3	44.3	2.9	8.6	—	—	—	70
New Byth	24.6	44.6	8.8	12.3	8.8	—	1.8	57
New Pitsligo	19.2	51.7	10.0	11.5	6.9	1.1	—	261
Sandhaven	18.7	62.5	—	6.3	6.3	6.3	—	16

Census of Population, 1851 Enumerators' books.

NEW VILLAGE, &c.

A New Village having, under proper regulations,
been laid out on the Eftate of STRICHEN, a
meeting is to be held in the houfe of John Glennie in
Redbog, on Saturday the 7th of April next, to give
off the firft twenty feus, at duties confiderably under
the remaining ones. The fituation of this village is
dry and healthy, moderately elevated, with an exten-
five tract of deep mofs adjacent, a great command
of fine fpring water, and fufficiency for driving mills
and machinery, lime ftone, and abundance of excellent ftones for building, to be found on the fpot.—
From the north-eaft to the weft of the village are
cultivated farms, naturally floping towards it; and, as
the leafes on thefe expire in a year or two, the
ground will be divided into convenient lots and parks
for the accommodation of the feuars. The propofed
turnpike road from Aberdeen to Fraferburgh, paffes
near faid village.

N. B. An excellent fituation for a Brewery, with
great command of fine water, to be let in Mormond
Village. For any further particulars as to the above,
apply to John Adamfon, factor at Strichen, or A.
Shirrefs, advocate in Aberdeen.

---

10. Newspaper advertisement for New Leeds, Aberdeenshire. (*Aberdeen Journal*, 27 March 1798)

in different streets from the artisans (as in Hopeman). These
broad patterns seem to have prevailed throughout the North
East and use of Census Enumerators' Books for the 1851 Census
shows that local migration persisted down to the mid-nineteenth
century (Table 4).

Conclusions and conjectures. The main findings of the research are
that the overwhelming majority of migrants travelled short

distances and largely comprised of tradesmen and labourers. In maritime villages, fishermen account for varying proportions of the population, generally in the range 25-60 per cent. This group tended to migrate longer distances than tradesmen. Both these patterns remained little changed from the period of the founding of the earliest villages in the 1750s to the final examples in the mid-nineteenth century.

The results presented in this chapter have mainly been derived from legal and estate papers. Ample sources exist to extend the analysis into the second half of the nineteenth century. In fact local historians would find migration to villages and the reconstruction of their demographic and socio-economic character a rewarding topic for study during an era when there were many new influences upon village life. It would be very interesting to discover the impact of the coming of the railway, changing demand for agricultural labour and the reduction of rural isolation. Suitable source material in the form of census data, trades directories and the files of local newspapers survives in abundance for such a study.

THE FISHERFOLK AND FISHING SETTLEMENTS OF THE GRAMPIAN REGION

James R. Coull

Introduction. Along no section of the British coast of equal length is there so high a frequency of fishing settlements as in the Grampian Region (Figure 1). Although relatively few of them have now much direct involvement in fishing, they testify to the fact that from pre-industrial times fishing here has been an important activity, and sea fish an important diet item. The big majority of these settlements are villages rather than towns, and some of them have been in existence for several centuries, although their peak of activity was in the earlier phases of the industrial age before fishing became concentrated at a few bigger harbours which provided the facilities required by modern boats. Now it is only exceptionally that there is much fishing activity in any of the villages; in the main they have become dormitory or retirement settlements, although fishermen frequently still constitute an important component of the population.

Records of the settlements. Apart from the county towns and royal burghs of Aberdeen and Banff, nearly all of these settlements were founded on coastal estates, but in general material relating to them in available estate papers is poor and often of late date: even on coastal estates the main concern was with farming rather than fishing. They also feature sporadically in a range of other sources, although many of these do little more than record the existence of particular settlements, and in the earlier records especially there is some bias towards places of burgh status rather than villages. Even among burghs, however, records are limited: along this coast there are twenty places that eventually acquired formal burgh status, but as elsewhere in Scotland burgh status not infrequently had limited significance. Most of these places never became more than villages in size or function. Hence although more is known about settlements like Aberdeen, Banff, Peterhead, Fraserburgh and Stonehaven, in many other cases burghs are on a common level with villages.

Estate charters are among the most useful documents for showing the earliest existence of the villages, and they also often figure on the earlier maps, from those of Timothy Pont (c. 1590) onwards. Local and district descriptions can give more information, and here the major sources are undoubtedly the compendiums of MacFarlane's *Geographical Collections* and the *Statistical Accounts*: even in these, however, coverage is variable and often cursory, and only rarely is there any real insight into the history or life of the settlements. Demographic and occupational data are occasionally available from parish registers, and Aberdeenshire has the unusual and relatively complete data of the Poll Book of 1696, although modern work has shown that this source has fairly serious under-reporting. For the later phases there is of course the detailed data of the original enumerations of the national Census from 1841 onwards. Other than the Census, the main other source of comprehensive information is that of the Fishery Board for Scotland from the early nineteenth century: here the villages tend to get occasional (as opposed to regular) recognition, prior to the reconstitution of the board in 1882 after which the published creek returns show annually the numbers of fishermen and boats, and the fish landings at each place.

In secondary sources, there are a number of local histories, journal and other articles which have been written over a period of more than a century, and some of the more recent ones are at the level of detail of individual villages. However the fullest and best study is undoubtedly the recent publication on the fishing villages of Buchan.[1]

In addition to documentary material, folk memory and tradition can be important and useful sources, although they have to be used with discrimination, especially for the period beyond living memory. These memories and traditions show most

11. Portknockie on a cliff-top site. The oldest part of the village is immediately above the harbour, which was constructed in the late 19th century; several phases of planned expansion are evident from the lay-out and types of the houses.

clearly that the way of life of the fishing villages developed to be distinct and apart from that of the landward areas. Moreover the villages each had traditions of their own, and conform to no stereotype.

Development of the settlement pattern. Other than the occasional archaeological evidence which covers a period of many centuries, the first definite references to fishing activity in this region are from the twelfth and thirteenth centuries and relate to

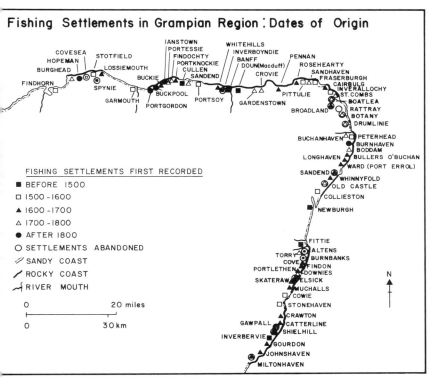

Figure 1.

salmon,[2] which were the species of greatest commercial importance during the Medieval period. At that time the fisheries for them were in the hands of burghs and religious houses, and royal burghs at river mouths like Aberdeen and Banff had a prominent involvement. Coastal villages had very seldom any role here before the nineteenth century. The fisheries for salmon were concentrated in the river estuaries as they entered them on their spawning runs, and it is very probable that the fishermen would also have engaged in sea fishing outside the salmon season. The first definite references to sea fishing are from the fourteenth century at Aberdeen and the Loch of Spynie (then

communicating with the sea), and Fittie (the fishing quarter of
Aberdeen) is on record in the previous century.[3]

As Figure 1 shows, at least eight places later known to be
active in fishing are known from the period before 1500, and in
one case (Down, later Macduff) it was specifically recorded as
a 'fish-town' as early as 1440.[4] If the limited character of the
record precludes any precise statement of the rate at which new
villages were founded, there was clearly a proliferation of them
and the majority were in existence by 1700. However the general size of village at this time remained small, as is most clearly
shown for those recorded in the Aberdeenshire Poll Book, where
it is evident that their manpower seldom extended beyond the
crews of three or four boats. The indications are that up to this
time the development of fishing represented mainly an addition
to local economies and food supplies on a limited scale; on
the other hand it is also clear that fishing had become firmly
established as a specialist occupation.

Villages continued to be founded in the eighteenth century,

12. Whinnyfold, in its cliff-top position above a steep shingle beach,
which had to be reached by steep paths. (Jim Livingston, Department
of Geography, University of Aberdeen)

and a few were set up even in the early decades of the nineteenth century before the modern forces of centralisation took a firm hold. However from the late eighteenth century the main emphasis was rather on the expansion of existing settlements, and during the improving movement this was done on a more planned basis than previously. New villages like St Combs and Hopeman were built in planned orderly rows, while it was common for existing settlements like Cullen, Portknockie and Portlethen to have planned extensions. It became fairly common in the nineteenth century for populations of individual villages to grow to several hundreds.

13. Newburgh on the Ythan Estuary. The age of this settlement is not certainly known, but it is one of the oldest involved in fishing. Both salmon in the river and white fish in the sea were caught. The oldest part of the settlement is on the peninsula extending into the estuary.
(Aerofilms, London)

If the general trend in the development of fishing settlement in the region has been that of proliferation and expansion, this was certainly not inevitable. Figure 1 shows a dozen places from which fishing has at some time been recorded, but which have not survived. The circumstances in which several of these were abandoned is obscure, especially when this happened before the late eighteenth century; this is the case, for example at Stotfield (Morayshire) and at Gawpoll and Elsick (Kincardineshire). It was always possible that the fortunes of settlements could be influenced directly or indirectly by changes in land ownership or in estate policy, and before the modern period small settlements could fail as a result of dearth. To this has to be added for the fishing villages the possibility of serious depletion of manpower through losses at sea: open-boat fishing in Scottish conditions was always a hazardous occupation, and in the earlier phases there were never more than a handful of boat crews in any village. In other cases it is clear that the village sites themselves were unfavourable, with difficult shores from which to operate and this was certainly a factor in the failure of settlements like Drumlinie and Botany in Aberdeenshire.[5] In the case of Altens and Burnbanks, established in the early nineteenth century on the coast south of Aberdeen to help provide fish for the city's rapidly growing population, what had been a favourable location near a big market became much less important; being close enough for fish wives to make the daily return journey on foot mattered much less once the railway arrived in 1849. In the case of Burnhaven, established at a rather difficult landing place immediately south of Peterhead in the 1830s,[6] the population very largely deserted it in the closing decades of the nineteenth century and settled in the town, in which the herring fishery was booming. All trace of the village was finally obliterated in the 1970s with the building of a new access road to the south side of the Peterhead harbour of refuge to serve the new oil bases.

Most striking of the settlements which were abandoned, however, are those that fell victim to geomorphological processes of coastal change. Changes have generally been greatest and most rapid on sand coasts, and it was this that was responsible at some point for closing off from the sea the former Loch of Spynie (already mentioned) and the Loch of Strathbeg. It has been

14. Burnhaven about 1880. The bigger boats in front of the houses are sailing herring drifters, pulled up off the beach in the off-season. The smaller boats at the top of the beach were used in lining for white fish.

possible to date the final closing off of the latter by a bay-bar to *c.* 1720,[7] and this had the effect of cutting off sea access from the former burgh of Rattray and the ferm-toun of Broadland, both still recorded as having fishermen in the Aberdeenshire Poll Book of 1696.[8]

Siting. The coast of the Grampian region consists of an alternation of rock and sand sections, and the marked preference for sites for fishing villages on the former is evident from Figure 1. In the days before harbours it was essential to have an adequate landing beach. Operation from shingle beaches on rock coasts was preferred, although working from sand beaches was not unknown, and indeed on the opposite side of the North Sea in Holland and Denmark there are numbers of fishing villages where the men had no option but to work from sand beaches. In addition to the obvious disadvantage for building foundations of

15. The village of Crovie. Although the site is much restricted at the cliff-foot, it was important to be near to the shore to reduce the work in carrying fish to the houses. Much of the work of line-baiting and cleaning fish was done in and around the home (Gordon Stables, Department of Geography, University of Aberdeen)

sandy terrain behind the beaches, there were a number of other disadvantages. Sand beaches are characteristically more open and without shelter, and as they are often more gently shelving there is a greater danger of waves breaking as they approach the beach; this renders the launching and beaching of boats more dangerous. In addition a boat pulled up on sand can more easily-bed down and become more difficult to launch. Although often appearing more forbidding, rock coasts have usually deeper water inshore and often have sheltered coves which make it easier to launch and beach the boats, and to load and unload them. The preferred situation of a shingle beach on a rock coast was the best for pulling up boats, and also the best surface on which to spread salted fish to dry.

As a general rule houses in a village were built near the shore, and often gable-end on to it to minimise the exposure to on-shore winds. Much of the work of line-baiting, gutting, cleaning and salting of fish was done in and around the houses, and it was an obvious advantage to minimise the carrying distance to the beach. However, there are considerable lengths of the rock coast which are backed by cliffs, some of which can reach well over 100 feet in height. On occasion, as at Pennan and Crovie, a village was built on a fragment of raised beach at the cliff foot; but more commonly as at Portknockie and Whinnyfold, the houses had to be built on the cliff top and access to the shore achieved by steep paths. The north Kincardineshire coast is one of the longest stretches of coast where this problem presented itself, yet there are a total of nine villages on the twelve-mile stretch between Cowie and Aberdeen.

Housing. In Lowland Scotland there are virtually no surviving examples of true vernacular housing, and this applies to fishing villages as well as to other settlements. Most of the older houses in them are examples of the two-roomed 'but and ben' structures with load-bearing walls, gable-end chimneys and windows which became general for much of Scottish society during the improving movement. While many of the oldest houses had originally earth floors and had thatch on their low roofs, no structures are on record with the older cruck frames. None of the deserted settlements have been dug by archaeologists, but the reported characteristics of Boatlea, the site of which was bull-dozed in the 1950s, were of a series of very small dwellings only a few yards long, and one surviving house in Broadsea (Fraserburgh) may approximate in form to these houses.

At the time of the improving movement there are many examples of landlords taking an interest in building a better class of house on their estates. They could give premiums to incoming fishermen as an incentive to build, as happened for example at St Combs,[9] and usually stipulated such details as house dimensions and walls constructed of stone and lime. The landlords might also undertake the building themselves, and put the houses up for let as happened for example at Botany and Buchanhaven.[10]

Earth-floored houses continued in use into the twentieth century, the practice being to sprinkle the floor periodically with clean sand which would be swept up and thrown out after it had become fouled. At a later stage, 'canvas' might be put down, this being an old boat sail which was used to cover the bare earth.

Intact housing of improving movement date is now a rarity, as most buildings have been improved by such means as building on extra rooms and raising roofs, as well as providing bigger windows and installing modern plumbing and electricity.

The fisherfolk and the land. Although substantially culturally apart for around two centuries or more, the fisherfolk of the north east are in origin substantially of a common stock with the landward population as the big common element in the dialect shows. As a general rule each fishing village had initially a small number of founding families: thus Boddam had its Cordiners, Sellars, Hutchinsons and Stephens; Gardenstown its Wests, Watts and Wisemans; and Portknockie its Mains, Woods, Slaters and Piries. Even now the numbers of surnames in many settlements are restricted and the use of 'tee-names' (nicknames) is frequent and indeed necessary to distinguish different families. However migration between villages was not unknown and new villages were generally initiated by recruiting fishermen from elsewhere already familiar with the work. It was also rare until the greater social mobility of the last generation for a fisherman to find a wife from other than another fishing family.

Despite the cultural separation of the modern period during which fishing has been substantially a full-time or nearly full-time commercial activity, there is evidence that at an earlier period many of the fisherfolk had a stake in the land, and produced part of their own requirements in such items as meal and milk. The fishermen who were among the first feuars at Peterhead at the end of the sixteenth century had a fifth of an acre each, with rights of pasturage and peat-cutting on the town moss;[11] and in 1683 Garden of Troup wrote about the farming practice of the fisher towns on the north coast of Aberdeenshire which included the cultivation of both oats and barley.[12] In the Aberdeenshire Poll Book (1696) five fishermen were enumerated at ferm-touns in the vicinity of Rattray while there were four others at Sandend in Cruden parish.[13] The siting of some fishing settlements at a distance back from the sea, such as Cove and Findon in Kincardineshire and Old Whinnyfold in Aberdeenshire is itself suggestive that fishing could have begun as a secondary activity in ferm-touns near the coast. Also as late as 1759 Down (the later Macduff) was a community of thirty-four crofter-fishers.[14]

The complete concentration on fishing evidently came earlier in some villages that others. Thus by the 1790s, the fishermen of Cairnbulg and Inverallochy were conspicuous as the only people in Rathen parish with no land,[15] but at the same date the fishermen at Portlethen and Findon in Kincardineshire had holdings of about an acre in size,[16] while at Whitehills in Banffshire the men had plots of $1\frac{1}{4}$ acres as late as 1840.[17]

With the increasing development of a commercial fishery there can only have been adjustments in the relations of the fishermen with their lairds, or with the tacksmen to whom fishings were let. The earliest arrangements on record show the men paying a single rent for house and boat, the boat being provided by the laird and shared by the crew, and the laird was bound to provide a new boat every seven years.[18] Such arrangements suggest that the fishermen were not tenants at will but had a secure tenure. It was also usual by the late eighteenth century in allocating the proceeds of fishing to give one share to the boat, as well as to each of the crew, to allow for maintenance and repair.

Early arrangements also show fishermen paying at least part

of their rents in fish, and in the towns of Peterhead and Fraserburgh there are also records of the payment of teind fish.[19] The
evidence is that by the end of the eighteenth century such
arrangements were in decline, and middlemen curers were more
and more taking on the organisation of the fishing. With the
big expansion which took place in the eighteenth century and
the re-orientation of effort to the herring fishery which required
bigger boats, curers became the main source of credit for
fishermen, as well as the buyers of the catch, and direct involvement of landlords become unusual.

The work of fishing. Fishing was a specialist occupation pursued
on a family basis: the men crewed the boats, but the women
made essential contributions in baiting the lines, and selling fish
in the hinterland. While there were variations in emphasis and
practice from one part of the coast to another, the main effort
was always directed at the catching of a range of white fish by
lines of different types. There was an intimate knowledge of the
fishing grounds within range of particular settlements and of
the species they might be expected to provide at different times
of the year.

The main type of boat in use was around twenty-five feet in
length, and was crewed by six men and sometimes a boy as
well; they could venture ten miles and more offshore and shoot
several miles of lines. The traditional boat types of the 'scaffie'
of the Moray Firth coast with its rounded stem, and the straight-
stemmed 'fifie' used elsewhere have been often noted,[20] but the
history of the building of such boats before the mid-nineteenth
century in Scotland is virtually unknown. These boats were
sufficiently heavy to require the efforts of more than their crew
to pull them up on the beach, and womenfolk might take part
although the task was very heavy. In the nineteenth century
when this fishing was at its peak it became common to install
hand operated winches behind the beaches to aid the drawing
up of the boats with a cable. They did have masts and sails,
although oars were also much used in their propulsion,
especially when hauling lines.

It was also usual for all settlements to have smaller four-man
yawls, which were mostly used for inshore fishing in winter for
haddock and codling, although they might also be used by older

men and boys at other times. By the end of the eighteenth century at the bigger centres of Peterhead, Fraserburgh and Buckie there was also some use of a bigger class of boat with two masts, and with crews of up to eight or nine men;[21] such boats might venture up to forty miles off and were used especially for the great-line fishing for cod and ling between March and June.

Open boat fishing in Scottish conditions was always cold work involving considerable discomfort as well as danger, and inevitably it was fairly frequently interrupted by adverse weather, especially in winter. Yet there was little option before the twentieth century but to fish when the weather permitted; sudden storms were always a particular risk, and periodic loss of life was one of the grim facts of experience.

Supplies of bait were essential for line fishing, and mussels were a main source of this, although lug-worm and sand eels were also used, while in winter recourse might be had to salted mackerel and saithe. Most shores had inadequate supplies of mussels by the time the position becomes fairly clear in the late eighteenth century, and supplies had to be imported from the main estuaries: these included the Ythan and Findhorn estuaries within the region, but they might also come from outside sources like the Montrose Basin and the Cromarty Firth and 'sown' on the local foreshores to be available when needed. Several hundred hooks would often have to be baited for a fishing trip, and this involved hours of prior work by the women, aided by the children, in collecting and shelling the bait as well as baiting. A significant illustration of this is that the school roll in the Aberdeenshire parish of Slains fell markedly in summer in the 1790s when everyone over six or seven years in the fishing villages of Collieston and Old Castle was occupied in line baiting.[22]

By the eighteenth century there was some diversification as well as expansion in the fisheries. At this stage Buckie alone had much involvement in the herring fisheries, by tradition due to men from Fife introducing the drift-net technique before 1700. It is a comment on the character of this fishery that even on a limited scale of operation, the men might make as much in a good six-week season as they did in the rest of the year,[23] although much labour was involved, and proper organisation

16. Fishermen dividing up mussels, used for line bait, at St Combs c.1880. Mussels were brought from the main estuaries, like the Ythan and the Findhorn, for this purpose. (Arbuthnot Museum, Peterhead)

and supervision of the work of curing was crucial. By the end of the century too there was an organised fishery for lobsters for the London market, and the then new technique of creel fishing had been introduced for the purpose. It was incoming English companies with their market contacts which stimulated this.[24]

Disposal of the catch. As a general rule the fishing villages provided an addition to the food supply in their immediate hinterlands. Much of the fish would have been consumed fresh, although preservation techniques are age-old and part of the catch was kept for out-of-season use, especially for winter. This involved gutting, splitting, and salting, followed by spreading out on shingle beaches and rocks to dry. It was usually the work of women and children to lay the fish out in dry weather and collect them in wet, and this might be done several times in the space of the month that it took to complete the curing of the fish.[25] Particularly well known here were the 'speldins' prepared at Collieston, long one of the most active villages, and able to capitalise on its relative proximity to Aberdeen. Short-term preservation by smoking was an important activity at some places, and probably best known here were the 'Finnan haddies' (Findon haddocks) from Kincardine-shire, where peat from mosses in the immediate vicinity was originally used in the smoking. Although traditional preservation methods have inevitably declined in the last century with year-round avail-ability of fresh fish, and more recently with domestic deep freezes, they have continued in use, if in a much reduced extent, to the present day.

Distribution in the local hinterland was an important role of the women folk, and the fish-wife was a kenspeckle figure in traditional Scottish life, who might cover distances of up to twenty miles or more in a long day carrying her creel, and exchanging fish for the meal, butter, cheese and eggs from the farming population. Even the coming of the railway did not displace the fishwife, and indeed could extend the range she covered: The Great North of Scotland Railway had special fish-wife concession fares which allowed the women to reach considerably greater distances from home.[26]

While this traditional sector of trade continued into the twen-tieth century, it is clear that by the end of the 18th century a

17. Fish wife with her creel, Collieston, *c.*1904. The fish in her hands
are probably 'speldins', whitings, which were salted and dried, and
were a well known product of the village. From C. L. Cutting, *Fish
saving. A history of fish processing from ancient to modern times.* (London,
1905)

larger-scale, more commercially-orientated sector had
developed, much of which was handled by merchants and
curers. The *Statistical Account* of the 1790s gives a series of values
and quantities which indicates this well, and suggests that at
least the stronger-going fishermen had relatively high living
standards, and were building up the capital which would allow
them to diversify and expand into the herring fishery in the
nineteenth century. Thus at Collieston the ling and turbot were
fetching 1s. each, while cod, skate and sole were all worth 6d.,[27]
and at Peterhead cod fetched between £1 and £1. 10s. per
dozen.[28] There was now an established outward trade,
especially with ports on the Forth and Tay, and from Whitehills

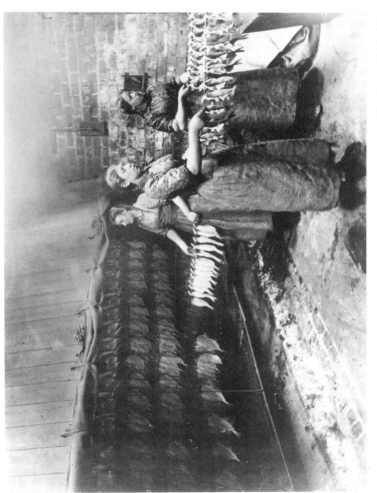

18. Women making 'finnans' (smoked haddocks) at Allan and Dey Ltd. in Aberdeen, 1911. (Aberdeen Art Gallery and Museums)

the annual value of fish sent out was between £500 and £600,[29] while Portsoy and Cullen between them despatched fish to the value of £840.[30] Salt from the Forth, needed for curing the fish, was an important return cargo. There was also a regular trade from Peterhead to London which took the form of 400 to 600 barrels of salt cod and haddock per year:[31] in winter when drying was largely precluded, the more expensive expedient of curing in barrels could be used, especially for a market with the purchasing power of the national capital.

Conclusion. Already before the eighteenth century closed there was appearing at the main harbours in the region some of the bigger scale fishing activities that were to become dominant. Peterhead and Fraserburgh had fitted out bigger boats to go to the summer cod fishing at Barra Head,[32] and the former had also established an interest in the Arctic whaling, which it shared to an extent with Aberdeen and Banff, and which was to be a main concern for half a century.

Nonetheless in the nineteenth century the villages continued to expand in population and in physical extent; and their fishing operations also continued to grow to a peak about the middle of the century. While fishing continued to be very much the dominant activity of village residents until after World War I, deep-seated changes were set in train by the development of the Scottish herring fishery which grew strongly throughout the century till it dominated the life of most of the Scottish fisherfolk—the men in drift-netting for the herring, and the women in gutting and net-mending. The latter was a major commitment, as the herring gear was as valuable as the boat for most of the century and sustained much wear and tear in use. From early in the nineteenth century the herring fishery was prosecuted with bigger boats which required harbours rather than landing beaches; and while some of the smaller places like Boddam and Cullen retained some direct involvement in it, it very much concentrated at Peterhead and Fraserburgh, the two main harbours on the North East shoulder which gave access to the biggest sea area.

Up to about the 1860s the main adjustment to this was that men from the villages went to the main ports to prosecute the herring fishery for the season from early July to early Sep-

19. Peterhead Bay in the early 20th century. The transition from sail to steam is illustrated by the presence of both sailing and steam drifters. (Arbuthnot Museum, Peterhead)

tember; they then returned home and resumed lining for white fish at other seasons. With overall success in the herring fishery boats increased in size and catching power, and in the second half of the century there was a strong incentive to extend their working year. This was achieved by something of a revolution in mobility.[33] They engaged in the early summer herring fishery in May and June in the Minch and at Shetland; in the autumn they went to East Anglia for a season that lasted into December. Various other fisheries were also followed around the British Isles, including those at Isle of Man, and both northern and southern Ireland. This new mobility was evident above all in the Buckie district; by the end of the century the Buckie men owned more herring boats than the men of any other Scottish district, yet were virtually never at home except between herring seasons.

In addition to the herring fishery, there was another major departure in the development of the trawl fishery for white fish, which concentrated at Aberdeen and distributed fish nationwide through the railway network. The trawl fishery began in 1882 and enjoyed thirty years of boom before World War I, and it largely displaced the traditional lining in open boats from the villages.

Although many villages did acquire piers or harbours in the late nineteenth century, these had a limited effect in countering the forces of centralisation—forces which from the 1880s were driven by auction markets for both herring and white fish in addition to a variety of other facilities available at the main ports. Exceptionally as at Gourdon and Whitehills, white-fishing has survived from active harbours: in the earlier part of this century this was possible by using motor-driven boats for lining, and more recently has involved the adoption of the ground seine and the light trawl. However these survivals serve mainly to emphasise the fact that fishing has largely been discontinued from other villages. The extent of continued involvement of other villages now varies. In virtually all cases at least some of the active fishing families have moved into the bigger centres over the last century and more. Villages in the Aberdeen orbit have very largely become dormitory settlements divorced from fishing. On the other hand, in the day of near-universal car ownership, it is a minor inconvenience for the many fishermen

20. Peterhead harbour. The two small off-shore islets which allowed the development of a safe harbour on this exposed coast are in the foreground. It came to the fore as a fishing harbour with the growth of the herring fishery last century, and now has become Britain's leading white fish port.

still resident in villages like Gardenstown and Sandend in Banffshire or Cairnbulg and Boddam in Aberdeenshire to maintain their homes in the traditional place while operating from bigger harbours—often at a variety of places in Scotland and indeed beyond.

REFERENCES

1. D.W. Summers, *Fishing off the knuckle. The fishing villages of Buchan* (Aberdeen, 1988).
2. J.R. Coull, 'Salmon-fishing in the North East of Scotland before 1800', *Aberdeen University Review*, xlii (1967), 31-8.
3. J.R. Coull, 'Fisheries in the North-East of Scotland before 1800', *Scottish Studies* 13 (1969), 17-32.
4. W.L. Cramond, *The Making of a Banffshire Burgh* (Banff, 1893), 2.
5. Summers, *Fishing*, 16-18, 23-8.
6. *New Statistical Account* [*NSA*], xii (Edinburgh, 1845), 381.
7. K. Walton, 'Rattray: a study in coastal evolution', *Scottish Geographical Magazine*, 72 (1956), 93.
8. W. Stuart, ed. *List of pollable persons within the shire of Aberdeen, 1696* (2 vols., Aberdeen, 1844), ii, 51, 54.
9. Summers, *Fishing*, 22.
10. Ibid., 24, 31, 32.
11. J. Arbuthnott, *An historial account of Peterhead* (Aberdeen, 1815), 18.
12. A. Garden of Troup, 'An account of the northside of the coast of Buchan 1683', Walter MacFarlane, *Geographical collections relating to Scotland*, ii (Scottish History Society, 1907). Edited by Sir A. Mitchell, 141.
13. Stuart, *List of pollable persons*, ii, 134.
14. Cramond, *Banffshire burgh*, 5.
15. *Old Statistical Account* [*OSA*] vi (Edinburgh, 1794), 15.
16. *OSA*, iv (Edinburgh, 1792), 454.
17. *NSA*, xiii, 237.
18. Coull, 'Fisheries', 24-5.
19. Ibid., 25.
20. e.g. P.F. Anson, *Fishing boats and fisherfolk on the east coast of Scotland* (London, 1930), 25-6.
21. Coull, 'Fisheries', 26.

22. *OSA*, v (Edinburgh, 1793), 284.
23. G. Hutcheson, *Days of yore* (1887), 18.
24. Coull, 'Fisheries', 27.
25. *NSA*, xiii, 338.
26. A.C. O'Dell, and K.Walton, *The Highlands and Islands of Scotland* (Edinburgh, 1962), 176.
27. *OSA*, v, 276.
28. *OSA*, xvi (Edinburgh, 1795), 549.
29. *OSA*, xix (Edinburgh, 1797), 307.
30. *OSA*, xii, 145.
31. *OSA*, xvi, 549.
32. Coull, 'Fisheries', 28.
33. J.R. Coull, 'The Scottish herring fishery 1800-1914: development and intensification of a pattern of resource use, *Scottish Geographical Magazine*, 102 (1986), 15-16.

THE PLANNED VILLAGES OF THE BRITISH FISHERIES SOCIETY

Jean Munro

The British Fisheries Society—or to give it its full title 'The British Society for extending the fisheries and improving the sea coasts of the Kingdom'—was an offshoot of the Highland Society of London, and concerned itself mainly with west and north Scotland. It was founded in 1786, in that period of new beginnings after the repeal of the post '45 repressive legislation. Since its foundation eight years earlier the Highland Society had collected quite a sum of money to be devoted to the practical encouragement of fisheries, and in the usual way of such bodies a committee was appointed to consider the best way to spend it. A number of factors contributed to the development of a separate Fisheries Society, but one very influential one was a lecture given to the Highland Society by John Knox, a London bookseller who had visited the Highlands many times and written on the subject.[1] He took the view that villages were essential for the co-operation needed for any successful venture, providing what Professor Smout describes as 'a framework for human life in the countryside', and producing a market. Knox proposed about forty villages of thirty to forty houses to be built along the coast between Arran and Dornoch. It was clear that few local landowners could find the money needed for such a scheme, and Knox thought that a joint stock company was the only solution. The committee of the Highland Society therefore turned itself into such a company, incorporated by Act of Parliament, and immediately began to collect promises of subscriptions.

Members of the Highland Society had already brought some parliamentary influence to bear during the long discussions over fishery legislation, which had been due for renewal in 1785. The acts of 1785 and 1786 were the results of a series of reports. The main change was that boat fishing was now to be encouraged by bounties paid on barrels of fish caught. Previously these bounties had been paid on tonnage, in order to promote larger vessels or 'busses', as used with success by the Dutch. A tangle of regulations was aimed at keeping these busses at sea for long periods with an eye to training seamen, and they were expressly forbidden to buy fish from local boats. The new law would stimulate the industry, because the barrel bounty was to be paid on results and not, as previously, paid in advance whether any fish was caught or not. Also the rule against busses buying fish from local boats was withdrawn, to the special benefit of the West Highlanders who could use small boats successfully in their sea lochs.

Before doing anything more concrete, the directors of the new British Fisheries Society tried some market research and sent out circulars asking, among other things, whether they should provide more help than houses and stores. The answers—thirty-seven of them—almost all came down in support of villages, although a few writers had reservations.[2] One Minch fisherman felt that the directors would be sinking money in houses which would never be occupied and proposed that

> in place of building houses for useless meckanicks, let the public aid be equally extended in assisting the strange fishers and poor natives along the coast. They know nothing of the act of sailing; let them be taught.

An example of his objections to Knox's theory of specialisation of trades concerned the making of nets:

> A netmaker's house would [likewise] be a superfluous expence because every married fisherman who brings a child of seven years of age to the coast settles a net maker theron and his wife and daughter are hemp spinners for net making.

There were others with practical experience, like the captain of the revenue cutter who said he would at any time rather sail fifty miles than write a sheet of paper. One landlord invited his reader 'to have a sea chart before him and for a moment to consider himself in a vessel standing northwards for the fishing grounds'. Another argued against 'sumptuous and numerous buildings' and felt that, as shoals were uncertain, the law should be changed to allow fishermen to land wherever they wished and set up tents (made from oars and sails, and not huts) free from any tax or duty. Many agreed that the main difficulty lay in inducing the people to inhabit the proposed towns and villages. But the provision of storehouses for salt and equipment was clearly essential and one writer suggested 'if floating stores could be contrived, it would probably be attended with more success'. It was stressed that, in the words of Lachlan Maclean of Torloisk, 'the merely building of villages will not be sufficient to enable the natives of this island (Mull) to begin the fishery. The poverty in which they are immersed makes it utterly impossible for almost any of them to purchase boats and tackle for the beginning of a voyage'. The wretched state of fishing materials, bad boats and want of skill were emphasised—'it is indeed incredible but a truth, that the only sail these nominal country fishermen use in general is a Highland plaid or blanket suspended 'twixt two oars and fastened by wooden pegs'.[3]

The emphasis on subsidies for buildings rather than boats and tackle came mainly from sad recent experience in the Highlands. In the 1750s a somewhat similar society had collected capital to build and equip busses. Whatever the truth about this venture, it left behind the impression that the main object of the society was to enrich its members, though Knox considered that it was mismanagement and lack of markets which caused the problems. In any case, that failure resulted in the British Fisheries Society being forbidden to undertake any trade and being restricted to buying land for leasing and building houses and stores by contract for renting. It did give loans for buying stock, but these had to be small and repaid with interest.

The Commissioners of Forfeited and Annexed Estates had also tried to help fisheries by establishing on their Highland estates groups of sailors demobilised after 1763. They gave subsidies towards the cost of boats and tackle, but found that this too led to disaster. The sailors were each to receive a bounty of £3 and a share of a boat rent free for three years, and those married also had a house and three acres of land rent free for seven years. Some of them took the bounty and were never seen again, and others fished for a few months and then (as one factor reported) 'eloped with boat, tackle and all'. So although it was clear that, as Dr Walker found on his tours of the islands,[4] there were plenty fish caught from the rocks for local consumption, there were no nets, few boats and no markets in the north west, and the payment of subsidies alone did not seem to be the answer. I have considered this in some detail because the matter has been debated ever since 1786, and in 1988 once again a writer has criticised the Society for the 'concentration of investment in a few villages, not necessarily the best fishing locations, where monies tended to be tied up in fixed assets such as buildings rather than advanced as working capital for boats and tackle'.[5] Whether the directors were right or wrong can never be proved, but the choice was not made lightly.

The location of the stations was the next problem for the directors. They felt that they should start with just two villages on the west coast, and agreed to have one south and the other north of Ardnamurchan. The outer isles already had Stornoway with customs house and store sheds, so the mainland and inner isles were to benefit first. A list of essential features was drawn up before parties of directors took off on visits to a variety of sites in the summer of 1787. Tobermory, offered partly by the Society's governor the duke of Argyll, was accepted quickly for its excellent natural harbour. Further north every sea loch was considered. Many were rejected because the local landowner already had projects at the planning stage if not on the ground; because there was not enough flat land avilable near a sheltered anchorage; because the owner would not co-operate; or in the case of Lochs Laxford and Inchard because the fish did not then seem to go there very often. The choice narrowed down to Loch Ewe and Loch Broom. The former was much liked, as it had a road to the east and the Stornoway packet left from there. But the best site, at Aultbea, was not available for sale, and the directors were certain that they could get a road built to Loch Broom (which they did) and change the route of the packet (though in fact it was not to leave from Loch Broom for nearly

200 years). Loch Broom was approved by visiting directors in summer of 1787 (some gave as lyrical a description as the best modern tourist) and Ullapool was considered almost ideal except that it was rather far from the open sea. The Society therefore bought the island of Ristol near the mouth, intending to build a storehouse there (though they never did).

It had been decided that a village in Skye would be considered later but the directors were very much impressed with Lochbay near Dunvegan, one saying that it was 'one of the first situations for a seaport town in Europe'. Their visit coincided with preparations for the departure of an emigrant ship, and in an attempt to offer the emigrants an alternative prospect they pushed forward the plans to purchase some land from MacLeod of MacLeod.

We will now have a brief look at each settlement to consider how it developed (or didn't).

ULLAPOOL was the first to start, had the most expended on it and for a time most nearly came up to the expectations of the directors. At the time of purchase in March 1788 there were fifty-seven acres arable, seventy-four pasture and nine hundred heath, moss and wood—and some of the latter was soon improved to pasture. The rough lay-out of the village was made by David Aitken, a surveyor from Tain (not Telford as is often supposed) and building was begun in June 1788.

This was a quick start and was later to be found too quick. The street fronting south was built at the wrong angle but allowed to stay; the inn was begun and had to be taken down as the plans had been changed. The pier was a disaster. Not properly surveyed, it gave continual trouble with silting up and too soft foundations, though it survived until 1854 and the present pier is on the same site. This is not the occasion to go into detail of the early years, but the public buildings (two storehouses, a shed for drying nets, a chapel, a schoolmaster's house, an inn, a pier and breakwater) were virtually completed in three seasons though a better school and a new church were added about 1830. In 1790 Ullapool was visited by Thomas Telford, who wrote a very detailed report[6] on the state of the buildings and made suggestions for improvement. The directors strove for a high standard of workmanship as an example to other village builders, and in places they got it—Telford commended the big storehouse (now Captain's Cabin) built by William Cowie of Tain. 'The masonry of the walls is I think the best I ever saw of the sort, and the carpenters and joiners work is, if possible, still better, in short I never saw better work in any building'—high praise indeed. The rest of the village failed to reach this standard—the inn was thought too expensive: though the builder was an industrious and honest man, a professional could have produced the same result for less money.

The rest of the public buildings were put up by one man, Robert Melville, who was to have an important place in the early history of Ullapool. He was the nephew of Robert Fall of Dunbar, whose fishery and commercial business had just gone bankrupt. He was keen to undertake work at Ullapool and by May 1788 had a contract to build houses, stores and curing sheds for the Society as well as a house for himself. A month later he arrived in Wester Ross with a number of fishermen, masons and other tradesmen. Melville was a hard worker and gave the settlement what it needed at first, but soon he was carrying on as if he was sole master of the place and was being called the Little Emperor of Ullapool. It was intended that he and others should supply or employ local fishermen, taking the financial risks that the Society was forbidden to do. In 1792 the Society gave him a loan to buy stock. But in 1793 he was attempting to charge the Society for more goods that he had ordered in England. Soon it became evident that he wanted no competition and made it impossible for rivals to use the Society's buildings. Several times the directors thought that they had attracted a competitor, but each one withdrew. However there were stations at Isle Martin and Tanera where settlers could sell their catch.

Because he was independent financially Melville did not supply details of his fishing, so we don't know how successful he was. It seems that the first few years were good and settlers did come to the village. Thirty-nine houses along the streets and as many thatched huts beyond the river were recorded in 1797. The real settlers each got a small garden and house plot, half an acre of arable at 10s. per acre and five acres uncultivated land at 1s. per acre, with repayment for enclosure and improvement. Also each had peat, stone, lime and sand free and the pasture for two cows. Loans were available for house building (of approved quality) but they were restricted to 50 per cent of the value and were payable only after the house was completed.

The fishing began to fail in the last years of the century but in 1800 Melville was still anxious to undertake a wet dock for ship building: he had at least one ship and in 1797 there were three ships belonging to Ullapool, perhaps all his. The directors felt that Ullapool was already costing too much and producing very little in rent, however, and refused the loan for the dock. But they made it clear that they would provide premiums for boats completed at the settlement. Melville was in trouble in 1802 and got a further loan, but in 1804 he was arrested for debt. In 1808 all his buildings were advertised for sale (the Society took them, and the stock later) and the following year he died. A successor seems to have been Murdoch Mackenzie, who had a loan to buy stock before 1804. In 1814 he was described as the principal fish curer and only ship owner in Ullapool, but two years later he was insolvent having lost, he said, £1,000 in mercantile concerns—probably not mainly fishing, which by now was very patchy on the west coast. The directors were still prepared to offer loans to attract professional fishermen and James Henderson of Clyth had one in 1826; but he was unable to set up a branch of his business in the west. So with ups and downs the fishing gradually declined, rents fell into arrears, meal had to be supplied to the settlers in bad years, and in 1847 the Society gave up the struggle and sold Ullapool for 5,000 guineas after having spent a total of £19,000 on the place.

TOBERMORY in north east Mull was the first choice of the directors. Not only was it offered by their governor the duke of Argyll and John Campbell of Knock, but it had a very fine natural harbour already well used for shelter. Boswell saw more than a dozen ships there in 1773 and was told that there could be as many as sixty to seventy in the bay together. The duke and his factor, James Maxwell, were rather more cautious than the enthusiastic starters at Ullapool. The village plan was to be somewhat similar, with public buildings near the shore line and dwelling houses above a rather steep bank. The first building was to be a storehouse and the obvious contractors were the Stevenson brothers, who had recently been the founders of commercial Oban. But Argyll was against power being in the same hands in both places, and persuaded a firm from Stanley near Perth to take on the storehouse. Stevenson did the other public building—the customs house, the inn and a breastwork to run along the shore in front of the houses. The customs house was in operation by 1791 and soon afterwards a regular thrice-weekly postal service was set up. Houses above the bank were taken slowly but steadily. The settlers were given similar portions of land as their fellows at Ullapool, but the contrast appeared at once in the fact that there were no fishermen listed among them, but rather merchants and dealers, and later shipmasters and mariners. As early as 1790 Maxwell had realised that Tobermory was too far from the fishing grounds for settlers to fish, as the directors had intended, in small boats—settlers 'will chuse to follow (the fishery) in the manner practised from the Towns in the Firth of Clyde: that is by means of larger vessels fit to navigate a sea agitated by frequent storms'.[7]

This is exactly what happened, and customs records show that as early as 1792 the vessels clearing out from Tobermory were engaged in coastal trade, though their cargoes did include fish as well as wool and kelp. The opening of the Crinan Canal, and later the Caledonian also, increased the mercantile import-ance of Tobermory. In its first ten years the expenditure at £4,032 was only about half that at Ullapool (mainly because no pier was needed until 1812), the rents were regularly paid and a profit was recorded. But all the same this was not really what the directors wanted. The trend continued and Tober-mory was not much affected by the collapse of the west coast herring fishery. Indeed the only complaint received from the settlers was over lack of grazing, and they cultivated their small portions of soil with a zeal which was commended to the inhabitants of Ullapool and Lochbay. Tobermory was sold in 1844, a vistor having summed up the position a few years earlier when he said that the town 'though very useful as a protecting haven and as a place of general commerce in a small way... has not, we understand, fulfilled as a fishing station the anticipations of its projectors'.[8]

LOCHBAY. As we have seen the directors moved out of their planned course to bid for Lochbay in Skye in 1788 in an effort to halt emigration. Unfortunately there were delays from the start of negotiations, as MacLeod himself was serving in India. By the time various misunderstandings were cleared up in 1790 many of the thirty-four who had early agreed to become settlers had cooled off, as they doubted the good faith of the directors and rumours flew round that the Society was to abandon Lochbay. The deal included a much greater proportion of good land than at either Ullapool or Tobermory, and much of the two farms which made up the settlement site had already been cultivated. Telford visited Lochbay in 1790 and planned the harbour, storehouse and inn.[9] But the Ullapool pier problems led to an abnormal amount of survey work in Skye, to prevent repetition of the problems experienced in the former place and the first contractor withdrew before he had begun. The local stone was found to be too soft for the harbour work and the distance from mainland ports made work expensive. A customs officer had to be picked up in Stornoway and taken to Skye to supervise unloading of cargo, and then presumably taken home again. Eventually in 1794 work began on the public buildings, and three years later Lochbay had store, schoolhouse, inn and pier. The latter was never satisfactory in spite of all the surveys and fell down 'with a great crash' in December 1815. In 1797 there were twenty-three settlers but apparently they were not fishermen, as two years later the Society was considering bringing men from Avoch or Nairn, and insisting that every settler must have at least a share of a boat. But it was too late—the herring had gone. However Lochbay was not the immediate tragedy it might have been as the fertile nature of the ground meant that settlers, having been given the same plots as at Ullapool, could live by their crofts alone and rents were paid until harvest failures brought more problems. But pasture remained adequate as the population rose very little in the early nineteenth century. Once again by 1822 rumours of a sale by the Society were rife but the directors delayed for a further fifteen years, refusing to give even a long lease as they did not want to expose their tenants to higher rents. In the end it was clear that Lochbay would never now make a fishing station and it was sold in 1837—the first to go.

PULTENEYTOWN. In his lecture to the Highland Society of London Knox had advocated villages from Arran right round to Dornoch, and the east coast was not entirely overlooked by the British Fisheries Society. Telford's tour of 1790 included a journey down the coast from Duncansby to Portmahomack to look at small harbours worthy of improvement. He found ten possibles, some already being used for fishing in a small way, but it was at Wick that he thought development should take place, based not on the existing town to the north but on flat land to the south of the river mouth. The land was bought in 1803.

Pulteneytown, as the station was called after a governor of the Society, developed rather differently from the western stations. First there was a subsidy from the Treasury of £7,500, from Forfeited Estates money, towards building the harbour, and a grant of £1,000 from the Commissioners for Highland Roads and Bridges, as half the cost of replacing the bridge over the Wick river. Then there was already some fishing based on the foreshore at Wick which carried on while the new station was being built. The whole of the new town was designed by Thomas Telford, taking the same general pattern of stores etc. on low ground and dwelling houses on the terrace above. From the start a much larger unit than elsewhere was planned— seventy-two house lots in the first place—and the settlers were not to be crofter-fishermen but full-time professional fishermen, who would make enough money to buy food from local farmers and the services of workers in other trades. The first curing lots—eleven of them—were sold by public roup in 1808 and houses were going up fast. Good fishing seasons brought more settlers. The pier was built according to plan, but the Society had continual trouble with the harbour—no sooner was it finished than it was too small as more and larger ships came in, and it was constantly filling up with sand. In 1823 a new outer harbour was designed, funded entirely out of harbour dues. Overcrowding ashore during the fishing season became a problem later, and in 1832 this brought the greatest set back to the town—cholera. By then the resident population was more than 2,000, where twenty-seven years before there had been only seven families.

Pulteneytown's development was almost independent of the

Society. The directors issued no instructions for improved agriculture or manufactures, and gave no loans for fishing or manufacturing companies or even to help settlers to build their houses, and they built no public buildings for rent. The Society's role was passive because no action was necessary other than to provide land and look after the harbour. Out of a total expenditure of £29,960 up to 1834, all but £900 was devoted to the harbour. Once this was built Pulteneytown was like a snowball rolling downhill, increasing in size and speed, with the directors required only to run along behind until they sold the settlement for £19,700 in 1892.

The British Fisheries Society made contributions to the fishing industry in other ways besides the villages. Their secretary had early claimed:

> If any law ought to be repealed or a new regulation adopted for the general benefit of the Fisheries, this Society will interest themselves for that purpose upon receiving information and proof upon the subject, and the directors of the Society, being members of both Houses of Parliament, there is little doubt of their success in every proper application to the Legislature. It is in short the Patronage of the Fisheries they have undertaken.[10]

This was a bold claim, but in the early years it had some truth. Most important was the work done to try to simplify the salt laws, which bore heavily on the poorer and more isolated fishermen, who found the complications of bonds, locked storehouses and customs clearance very oppressive. The directors won several minor but useful concessions before 1800. They continued to lobby Parliament and at least eight of them sat on a committee of twenty-six set up in 1801 to consider the whole question, and which recommended total abolition of duty on salt. This did not happen until 1825, but the Society was continually bringing complaints to the authorities until it was done. Similar influence was used to increase the number of special officers or justiciary bailies, whose job was to keep the peace among fishermen, and to strengthen their authority. This was done by the directors collecting evidence of the need for such action on behalf of the fishermen, and presenting it to the appropriate authorities. In 1808 the act which set up the Fishery

Board also provided for a naval officer to be superintendent of deep sea fishing, and in 1815 another was appointed for the coastal and loch fisheries.

Another grievance was the importation of foreign (mainly Swedish) herring through Ireland into the West Indies at a lower duty than was possible from Scotland. The West Indies was one of the most important markets for British fish, especially as duty-free salt was available for exported fish only at that time, and not yet for the home market. The case was presented by the Society to the Treasury in 1790 and soon the duty payable in Ireland was adjusted and the abuse was removed.

After the Fishery Board was established in 1809 the Society appears to have chosen to be nothing more than a private association of subscribers, leaving the Board to undertake the 'patronage of the fisheries'. In this limited role the Society carried on until 1893, by which time the Crofters Commission was advocating a programme very similar to that of the Society nearly one hundred years before. More recently, in 1967, the Highlands and Islands Development Board introduced its first report by acknowledging that 'there has been dissatisfaction with past policies although that by no means proves that all or even the majority of these policies were fundamentally wrong. Some may indeed have been wrong only in time and scale'.[11] The success of Pulteneytown is now recorded in a local museum, while Tobermory and Lochbay went on as expected—the one as a commercial centre and the other as a sprawl of small agricultural holdings. Only at Ullapool have changing conditions brought about its rebirth as a fishing station, thus justifying some of the Society's planning.

REFERENCES

1. John Knox, *A discourse on the expediency of founding fishing stations* (London, 1786).
2. National Library of Scotland, MS 2619 and Scottish Record Office [SRO], GD9/3/49ff. Extracts of answers to the British Fisheries Society 1786-7. Also see article 'The British Fisheries Society: 1787 questionnaire', *Northern Scotland*, ii (1974-7), 37-55.

3. ibid.
4. John Walker, *Report on the Hebrides*, ed. M.M. Mackay (Edinburgh, 1980).
5. A.I. Macinnes, 'Scottish Gaeldom: the first phase of clearances', *People and society in Scotland*, i, *1760-1830*, ed. T.M. Devine and R. Mitchison (Edinburgh, 1988), 82.
6. Telford report in SRO, GD9/3/583ff.
7. Maxwell in SRO, GD9/3/629.
8. James Wilson, *Voyage round the coasts of Scotland* (2 vols., Edinburgh 1842), i, 173-4.
9. SRO, GD9/3/577.
10. SRO, GD9/8/136.
11. HIDB *First Report*, 1. The papers of the British Fisheries Society are in the Scottish Record Office, reference GD9. A more detailed account of the Society will be found in Jean Dunlop, *The British Fisheries Society 1786-1893* (Edinburgh, 1978).

THE RISE AND FALL OF MANUFACTURING IN RURAL ABERDEENSHIRE

Robert E. Tyson

Until recently the majority of people who lived in rural Aberdeenshire earned their livelihood from agriculture, but there were always surprisingly large numbers employed in other sectors of the economy. In the nineteenth century, for example, each burgh and village still had its tradesmen (tailors, boot and shoemakers, saddlers, wheelwrights, blacksmiths etc) who served the needs of the local community, as did their counterparts in the seventeenth and eighteenth centuries. The latter, unlike those in the nineteenth century, lived mainly in the innumerable ferm-touns, which were scattered across the face of the countryside until swept away between 1780 and 1830 by agricultural improvement, and grew much of their own food. Living alongside them were numerous men, women and children who also combined manufacturing with agriculture, but the goods that they produced were destined mainly for sale beyond the North East of Scotland.

Rural Aberdeenshire before the nineteenth century was a major manufacturing centre and an example of *proto-industrialisation*. This word (derived from Greek *protos*, meaning first) began to be used in the early 1970s to describe traditionally organised cottage industries which, as a result of the expansion of trade, specialised in making textiles and other goods for national and international markets.[1] Such cottage industries were found in many regions of Britain (e.g. East Anglia, the

West of England, the West and North Ridings of Yorkshire, East and North Wales) and throughout Europe. In Scotland, Aberdeenshire was probably the main area of proto-industrialisation for most of the period under discussion, and yet by the middle of the nineteenth century its cottage industries had largely disappeared. The purpose of this essay is to examine the rise and fall of these industries and to explain why they should have been so prevalent in Aberdeenshire.

I

There were two principal cottage industries in rural Aberdeenshire: the weaving of woollen cloth and the knitting of worsted stockings. We know hardly anything about the sale of either in the home market but Aberdeen began to export plaiding (a coarse, twilled cloth made from carded wool) from 1580 onwards. Exports in 1610-14 averaged only 13,000 ells a year (an ell is thirty-seven inches), but from then onwards there was rapid if erratic growth. In 1620-4 exports were 40,000 ells a year, in 1630-4 63,000 and in 1635-9 93,000. The peak year was 1639 when no fewer than 121,000 ells left Aberdeen for the Netherlands, the Baltic and northern France.[2]

The figure for 1639 was probably never reached again. What few statistics are available for the post-civil war period suggest a considerable decline since the 1630s: 73,000 ells in 1650-1, 62,000 in 1668-9 and 72,000 in 1669-70. It was from the mid-1680s onwards, however, that exports really began to collapse.[3] Alexander Skene of Newtyle, a prominent Aberdeen merchant, wrote in 1685 that plaidings and fingrams (a coarse serge made from combed wool, which had begun to be exported earlier in the century) were selling at only half their former value and 'neither is the half exported'.[4] Worse was to come. By the beginning of the eighteenth century cloth exports were said to be only a quarter of what they had been earlier and, more specifically, fingrams only one-sixth. Although there are no comparable statistics for sales within Scotland, these were badly

hit by the appalling famine of the 1690s, since high food prices
left little money to spend on clothing.[5]

In part the collapse of cloth exports was due to war, first with
the Dutch and then the French, which seriously interrupted
trade, while the loss of the Dutch plantations in Brazil, the
ultimate destination of many of the fingrams sent to the Netherlands, was another blow. Contemporaries also blamed what
Skene called 'deceitful mismannadgment', the numerous frauds
constantly perpetrated by the weavers, the inadequate skills
of the labour force and the generally inferior wool were probably more serious problems. The result, as with most Scottish
exports, was a poor quality product which was acceptable only
because of its low price. This made the industry vulnerable to
competition from an infant woollen industry such as that of
Sweden, which could soon produce an acceptable alternative
made with even cheaper labour.[6]

There is general agreement that the export of Aberdeenshire
cloth came to an end sometime during the first half of the
eighteenth century, though the absence of trade figures makes
it impossible to fix a firm date. The demise probably took longer
than is generally recognised, particularly as the lighter fingrams
may have found a new market in the British colonies, but by
1750 it was complete. The home market seems to have held up
better for a time, and although servant girls stopped buying
fingrams for their gowns, a variety of other cloths, including
duffles, serges, seys, and linsey-wolseys or winceys was still being
produced in the 1790s. Long before that date, however, worsted
stockings had replaced woollen cloth as the principal export of
Aberdeen.[7]

Stockings began to be exported in the early seventeenth
century, mainly to the Netherlands and the Baltic, but the
quantities appear to have been modest until the eighteenth
century. When regular statistics became available from 1743
onwards, Aberdeen was shipping out over 200,000 pairs a year,
but the most rapid growth came from the 1770s onwards and
in 1793 no fewer than 900,000 pairs were exported, most of
them to northern Europe, though there was also a substantial
trade with Portugal and North America. The value of these
exports in 1782 was estimated to be £110-120,000 while a few
years later Thomas Pennant put them at £104,000. The most

accurate figure is that of £103,000 for 1795 in the *Statistical Account*, but exports in that year were little more than 200,000 pairs.[8]

The key to the rise of these two export industries was the relationship between a small section of the Aberdeen merchant community and the rural population. Although Aberdeen in the 1630s had perhaps 350 merchants, not more than seventy-five of them traded abroad. The export trade in stockings was similarly controlled by a small group (in 1771 there were twenty-two mercantile houses involved) whom James Loch, himself a merchant as well as the General Inspector of Fisheries in Scotland, called 'the best merchants in Scotland'.[9] There were weavers in Aberdeen and adjacent Old Aberdeen but they were few in number (the Aberdeenshire Poll Book records the names of twenty-nine in each burgh in 1695) and they probably produced better quality, dyed cloth for local consumption.[10] The weaving of cloth, therefore, was carried out almost entirely in the countryside, and although the knitting of stockings was more likely to be found in Aberdeen, where it may well have originated, it too was a predominantly rural industry.

Several references to both industries in their early days suggest that they were organised under the *verlaggsystem* or putting-out system. Thus Thomas Garden, an Aberdeen tailor and deacon-convener of the incorporated trades in 1627-8, is said to have had an extensive sheep farm just outside the burgh and to have employed large numbers of weavers whom he supplied with wool. Similarly, George Pyper, who was admitted as a guild burgess in 1648, is supposed to have given employment and credit to 400 spinners and knitters in the countryside. These examples, however, are probably untypical since the *kaufsystem*, whereby the workers provided their own raw materials and sold their products locally, prevailed in the cloth industry until its demise, and in knitting up to the middle of the eighteenth century.[11]

The Aberdeen Dean of Guild Court prohibited merchants from buying cloth and stockings directly from the households that produced them. Instead, in an attempt to prevent abuses, all goods intended for export were supposed to be inspected and stamped before being sold at local fairs and markets either to the Aberdeen merchants themselves or to middlemen who took

them for sale in the royal burgh. In practice it proved impossible to enforce these regulations, even when supported by act
of Parliament, and there are numerous cases of forestalling in
the records that have survived. For example, in 1624 George
Ricard, merchant and Aberdeen burgh treasurer, was fined
twenty merks for 'bringing of great quantities of plaiding before
the same is presentit to the mercat'.[12]

The concern about the poor quality of Aberdeenshire's
textiles, which contemporaries regarded as the most important
factor in the collapse of cloth exports, helps to explain the
adoption of the *verlaggsystem* for the knitting of stockings after
about 1750 and the subsequent end of the Dean of Guild Court's
efforts to regulate the industry. Previously the wool was produced either in the knitter's own immediate area or, particularly
in Aberdeen, was brought from upper Deeside for sale in wool
markets; merchants even encouraged local farmers to breed and
keep sheep until they were five or six years old for the sake of
their wool. However, there were numerous complaints about
the quality of the wool, which came from sheep smeared with
tar to protect them during the winter, and lack of skill in
combing it. The Aberdeen merchant-hosiers now began to
import wool from Newcastle and London, which they had
combed in their warehouses. By the time of the *Statistical Account*,
over 600,000 lbs of wool with a value of £22,500 was imported,
and there were nearly 400 wool combers in the burgh. According to Pennant, only 2,000 pairs of stockings were now made
with Aberdeenshire wool. The result was a dramatic reduction
in the number of sheep kept there; George Keith in his *General
view of agriculture in Aberdeenshire* (1812) claimed that at the time
of writing there were only 100,000 compared with 600,000 in
1690 and 300,000 in 1780, with most of the decrease taking
place in the lower areas of the county.[13]

Instead of simply purchasing the stockings, the merchant-
hosier, or more usually his agent, 'came to different stations
every four weeks and gave out their wool, which they received
knitted into stockings. Thus the makers are not put to the
trouble and expense of providing raw materials for their work
but receive their wages punctually when their work is done.'[14]
The switch, as well as improving the quality of the stockings,
gave the merchant-hosier greater control over the knitters. It

also eliminated the need for middlemen and the use of traditional fairs and markets.

II

In 1624 the burgh commissioners complained to the privy council of Scotland about the high price of wool and claimed that
20,000 people in the North East earned their living 'by the
making of plaids'.[15] Like most contemporary estimates, this
figure should not be taken too seriously, but it does indicate that
the cloth industry was already regarded as a major employer. In
1695, when the export of cloth was in terminal decline, the
Aberdeenshire Poll Book gave the names of 1,299 weavers,
including those in Aberdeen and Old Aberdeen, out of a total
of 3,440 tradesmen. No distinction was made between linen and
woollen weavers, or between those who wove cloth primarily
for domestic consumption and those who specialised in plaidings
and fingrams for export, while in sixteen of the eighty-nine
parishes, no distinction was made beween the various trades.
Even more serious, there was large-scale tax evasion. I have
argued elsewhere that as many as 30,000 adults who should
have paid the tax are missing from the lists and many of them
would have been weavers. Moreover, the Poll Book omits the
occupations of women other than those who were tenants and
servants, even though they made up the greater part of the
industrial labour force in the countryside.

    There is, however, a better source. In 1729 the Aberdeenshire
Justice of the Peace compelled every fingram weaver to sign a
statement promising to weave cloth that was of good quality
and the correct dimensions. In all 633 statements have survived,
and such was the care taken to ensure that every fingram weaver
signed either his name or his initials, it is likely to be a fairly
reliable total.[16] Since fingrams were light, coarse fabrics and
probably exported undyed, the ratio of combers and spinners
to weavers was probably only six to one which would give a
total labour force of not more than 4,500. This was a much
smaller figure than in the 1630s, when the cloth industry was
at its height, and it was probably surpassed by the numbers
employed in knitting.

In 1795 it was claimed that the latter employed 30,000 occasional workers in Aberdeenshire and the adjacent part of Kincardineshire, at a time when the combined population of both counties was just under 147,000. Since knitting was predominantly a part-time occupation, with even a skilled pair of hands producing not more than three pairs of stockings a week for which they earned not more than 2s.–2s. 6d., this figure of 30,000 is certainly not an exaggeration. The same source reckoned that £77,000 was paid out in wages in that year (almost certainly less than in the peak year of 1793) and that the average weekly wage was 1s. 6d., which suggests that at least 20,000 people knitted for export.[17] There was also an unknown but probably substantial output of stockings for sale in Great Britain.

Who were these weavers and knitters? The Poll Book gives the names of 3,440 tradesmen (who were probably representative of weavers), of whom only 232 (6.7 per cent) were also tenants, and their average rental of just of £11 was only one-third the mean for the 6,000 tenants in the Poll Book. It is clear that the great majority of tradesmen, including weavers, came from the ranks of the remaining rural population, particularly sub-tenants (i.e. cottars and grassmen) who provided tenants with labour in return for land and grazing. In the parish of Cruden, for example, only one of the thirty-two weavers was a tenant, six were more described as sub-tenants or cottars, and twenty-one were grassmen. In Huntly parish one weaver was a tenant and the remaining twenty-five were cottars.

Although sub-tenants probably formed the majority of those living in the countryside, we know very little about them. Malcolm Gray has described them as people who 'had no firm position in society, no fixed occupation, no definite tenure of land; they were not specifically farmers, wage-earners or independent craftsmen but all three at once'.[18] Such people were very dependent upon their trades for part or even most of their livelihood since the land that they received from the tenants was insufficient to keep them and they needed money to buy food and other necessities. It is probable that in many ferm-touns the majority of families had by-occupations; in Arnhead in the parish of Turriff, for example, the nine households listed in the Poll Book had eight weavers between them. A few tradesmen, especially those with apprentices, may have been full-time industrial workers but most would have had at least a kale-yard; in the parish of Aberdour, only three out of the fifty-nine tradesmen there in 1793 were landless.[19] It should be emphasised, however, that the bulk of the labour force involved in the production of cloth was made up of women and children who prepared and spun the wool before it was woven by the men, and that the household was the unit of production.

The production of stockings was even more dominated by women. Some were knitted by young boys and old men, par-ticularly during the winter months when there was no herding of livestock, but most were made by females from the age of seven upwards. A number of contemporary accounts describe them spinning (with the rock and spindle) and knitting, even when tending livestock in the fields or walking along the roads, though some ministers complained that these were unhealthy, sedentary occupations. In some parishes knitting appears to have become almost a full-time occupation, particularly when crops failed, as in 1782-3, and it was necessary to increase earnings. In these parishes, except perhaps at harvest time, the work of the land was done by the men, and the knitting by the women, there being a strict division of labour between the sexes. It is probable, however, that for most women elsewhere knitting was a part-time occupation, particularly in coastal parishes such as Nigg which lay immediately to the south of Aberdeen. There the women knitted when they were not gathering dulse, collecting and burning kelp, selling fish inland, digging peat, harvesting, or carrying out household duties.[20]

The females of every class appear to have knitted, including the wives, daughters and female servants of tenants, but con-temporary accounts singled out those of crofters, for without the money that they received '... the rents of the small crofts could not be paid, as the crofters had no other way of earning money, but by annually rearing a young ox or cow'.[21] It was claimed that in some parishes half or more of the rent was earned in this way. Francis Douglas, describing north Kin-cardineshire in 1782, wrote

> You see everywhere numbers of poor huts and starved cattle
> [but] ... poor people have special inducements to settle in this

district. They have peat and turf in great abundance, they are
on the sea coast, and they can at most seasons have fish reasonably; they have a superabundance of stone for building their
houses, and there are some pinewoods in the neighbourhood
where they can purchase timber from them; and what is still of
greater consequence, being within a few miles of Aberdeen, the
females have constant employment knitting stockings to the
manufacturers. By their unremitting labour in this branch, they
earn money to pay their rents, and by keeping one or two cows,
and raising a little grain, they are enabled to live in a humble
but contented way.[22]

The increase in earnings from knitting as exports grew was
probably a factor in the gradual transition towards the payment
of rents in money, though stockings were sometimes accepted
in lieu of cash, and there was thus every incentive for landlords
to encourage the industry. The larger tenants benefited since
they were assured of a more plentiful supply of labour from
their sub-tenants, who could live partly off their earnings of
their wives and daughters. Without these earnings, the countryside would have been unable to support such a large population.

III

Cottage industries thrived in rural Aberdeenshire because
abundant supplies of cheap labour, the most important factor
of production, were readily available, perhaps more so in
relation to resources than in any other part of Lowland
Scotland. The twenty-five predominantly Lowland counties
(including Perthshire) had an average of 3.1 acres per £ Scots
valued rent at 1674 but the ratio for Aberdeenshire was 5.4
acres per £. Only Banffshire, Dumbartonshire and Nairn were
higher, and the mean for seven of the twenty-five counties was
actually lower than the 1.9 acres per £ for Logie-Buchan, which
had the lowest ratio of any Aberdeenshire parish. Again, if the
valued rent for each county is divided by the first available
population figure, that for 1755 (less the population of the four
leading Scottish cities of Edinburgh, Glasgow, Aberdeen and

Dundee), Aberdeenshire held bottom position with a valued rent of only £2.2 per person compared with a mean for Lowland Scotland of £3.7.

Aberdeenshire had the largest area of arable land in Scotland but much of it was of poor quality, and this, together with climate and topography, produced an environment that could be cruel; in the famine of 1695-9 the population may have fallen by as much as 20 per cent.[23] It was also one of the last areas of Lowland Scotland to improve its agriculture, and yet in 1755 Aberdeenshire had more inhabitants than any Scottish county except Perthshire, and was home to one Scotsman in eleven. The great majority of them lived in the countryside since, apart from Aberdeen, there was little urban development. In 1755 Old Aberdeen and Peterhead were the only burghs other than Aberdeen with more than a thousand inhabitants. Few farmers actually owned land (in 1667 there were 621 heritors, who had been reduced to only 250 in 1771)[24] and most tenants held leases of five years or less on onerous conditions. Below them, as we have seen, was a mass of near landless sub-tenants and others who had no land at all.

The consequences of all this was abundant, cheap labour. Alexander Skene described the failure of an Edinburgh merchant to produce plaidings there as cheaply as in the North East because 'the people that wrought their Plaiding [in Aberdeenshire] had not by far such entertainment as his servents had, and ... they drank their clear spring water than ale; and therefore they had their Plaiding much cheaper than he had his [in Edinburgh]'.[25] Certainly the money-wages of servants and agricultural workers appear to have been lower than elsewhere. Recent research has revealed that those of Aberdeenshire male servants in the 1690s were only 59.9 per cent of those in Renfrewshire and of female ones only 49.7 per cent. Although the gap was narrower a century later, Aberdeenshire was still a low wage area.[26] These differences may in part have been the result of a larger non-wage element in Aberdeenshire and in any case only a minority of people actually received wages, but they are probably a reasonable indication of earnings that were low even by the standard of contemporary Scotland. Nevertheless, this agriculturally backward, poor region was dominated by the wealthy royal burgh of Aberdeen with its large and dynamic merchant class. These were ideal conditions for cottage industries.

Such industries, however, were not spread evenly throughout the countryside. In the Poll Book there were few tradesmen in the Highland parishes, particularly the Gaelic speaking ones of upper Deeside, although they were the poorest in Aberdeenshire and contained numerous small tenants who produced abundant supplies of wool but insufficient food to feed themselves (see Figure 1). Imports of grain were purchased with money from the sale of cattle and wool, and although there was a small linen industry after 1750, the main by-employment was the illicit distilling of whisky. This failure to develop a large textile industry when conditions, according to proto-industrial theory, were apparently ideal is puzzling. Lowland contemporaries put it

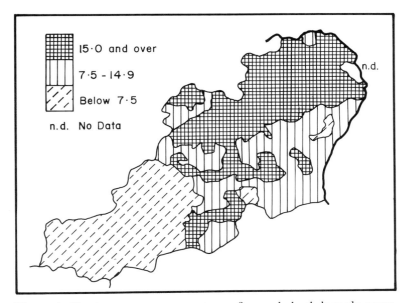

Figure 1. Tradesmen as a percentage of recorded adult male population, Aberdeenshire (including Aberdeen and Old Aberdeen), Aberdeenshire, 1695. Source: J. Stuart (ed.), *List of pollable persons within the shire of Aberdeen, 1696* (2 vols., Aberdeen 1844). The list was largely compiled in September 1695.

down to the laziness of the men, which is hardly an explanation
since the manufacture of textiles depended mainly upon the
supply of female labour. Differences in language and distance
from Aberdeen may have been more important, though as
regards the latter, wool from upper Deeside was sent to Aberdeen and grain for the distilling imported from the coastal
plain.[27]

The remainder of Aberdeenshire can be divided into two
distinct regions. The first, roughly triangular in shape, consisted
of the parishes surrounding Aberdeen, and the more fertile ones
(usually with fewer than 3.5 acres per £) between the lower
reaches of the Don and the Ythan rivers and along the coast as
far north as Peterhead. This region, most of which coincided
with the ancient territorial division of Formartine, had many
tradesmen but they served mainly local needs, while in the

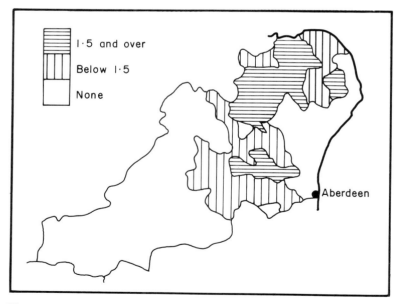

Figure 2. Fingram weavers (1729) as a percentage of population
(1755), Aberdeenshire. Source: Aberdeen District Archives, Weavers'
Enactment Books, i and ii; J.G. Kyd, *Scottish population statistics* (The
Scottish History Society, 1952), 52-5.

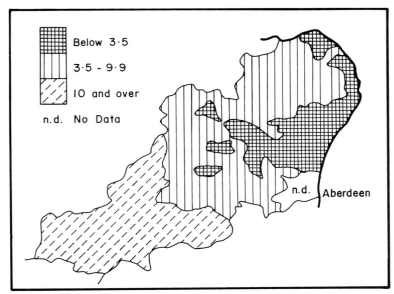

Figure 3. Acres per £ valued rent, Aberdeenshire (excluding Aberdeen area), 1674. Source: A. and H. Tayler (eds.), *The Jacobite cess roll for the county of Aberdeen in 1715*. (Third Spalding Club, 1932)

coastal parishes fishing provided an alternative to agriculture. To the north and west lay the second region, where tradesmen in the Poll Book were more numerous (in some parishes they were a quarter or more of recorded males) and where *all* the fingram workers of 1729 were to be found. The latter were particularly numerous in the interior of northern Buchan, the 'cold, hard shoulder of Scotland', where great stretches of muir and moss surrounded the small, irregular fields, and, to a lesser extent, in a belt of parishes which lay to the south of the Don and Urie rivers (see Figures 2 and 3).

The contrast between the two regions can be seen by comparing the fifteen parishes where fingram weavers in 1729 were 1.5 per cent or more of the population in 1755 with the same number to the south and east, which had none at all (see Table 1). The latter had a much higher ratio of valued rent to acreage, a higher rent per tenant, and a somewhat greater proportion of single tenant farms (usually regarded as evidence of greater commercialisation than joint-tenancies). There were also more servants per household but far fewer herds, and the wages of both servants and herds were considerably higher than in the parishes with fingram weavers; wages were particularly low and herds most abundant in northern Buchan, the heartland of cottage industries. These differences are a reflection of differing geographical conditions, particularly in soil types, which meant that although both regions had the infield-outfield system with its mixed agriculture, the more fertile non-weaving parishes concentrated more on commercial grain production and the weaving ones on subsistence agriculture and the rearing of livestock. Much of northern Buchan, for example, was given over to sheep farming, while large flocks grazed on the common land of Kintore, a weaving parish to the south of the Don.[28]

If the Highland area is ignored, this seems to support the general view that cottage industries were found mainly in relatively infertile areas of pastoral and/or subsistence farming where the inhabitants had more incentive and time to engage in by-employment. However, this does not apply to the hosiery industry. The knitting of stockings appears to have begun in and around Aberdeen and then spread north to Formartine, where there were no fingram weavers, and south to adjacent Kincardineshire as far as Inverbervie, two agriculturally contrasting areas since North Kincardineshire was very much like Buchan. When cloth exports collapsed in the first half of the eighteenth century, it is probable that stocking manufacture then moved into the weaving parishes, with the exception of those in northern Buchan, which instead turned to linen. Stockings were eventually made, therefore, almost everywhere within a thirty–thirty-five mile radius of Aberdeen, an area that more or less coincided with the area controlled by the Aberdeen merchants in 1750 (see Figure 4). The northern part of Buchan was now dominated by the small but growing ports of Banff, Fraserburgh and Peterhead, while South Kincardineshire, which formed an extension of the Angus linen industry, lay within the hinterland of Montrose.

The reason why the knitting of stockings, unlike the manufacture of plaidings and fingrams, was not confined to areas of poor soils with predominantly pastoral or subsistence agri-

TABLE 1

Weaving and non-weaving parishes (1729) in Lowland Aberdeenshire

	(a) Parishes with no[1] fingram weavers	(b) Parishes where[2] more than 1.5 per cent of population (1755)	(a) as a percentage of (b)
Valued rent per acre (1674)	£0. 7.0[3]	£0. 4.1	170.0
Valued rent per tenant (1695)	£45.15.2	£38.10.0	118.9
Percentage of single tenant farms (1695)	72.8	64.5	112.9
Servants per 1,000 households (1695)	530	393	134.9
Herds per 1,000 households (1695)	34	123	27.6
Servants and herds per 1,000 households (1695)	564	516	109.3
Annual mean wage per male servant (1695)	£11.14.7	£10. 5.0	114.4
Annual mean wage per female servant (1695)	£7.19.0	£6.10.0	130.3
Annual mean wage per herd (1695)	£5. 8.5	£3.14.5	145.7

[1] Belhelvie, Crimond, Cruden, Drumoak, Ellon, Foveran, Logie-Buchan, Methlick, New Machar, Newhills, Old Machar, Peterhead, Slains, Tarves and Udny: combined population 26,545 (1755).

[2] Aberdour, Auchterless, Dyce, Fyvie, Inverurie, Kemnay, Kinnellar, Kintore, Longside, Monquhitter, Monymusk, New Deer, Strichen, Turriff and Tyrie: combined population 19,123 (1755).

[3] All monetary figures in £Scots = 1s.8 sterling. Valued rent per acre (1674) excludes Newhills and Old Machar because of insufficient data.

Sources: Aberdeen District Archives, Weavers' Enactment Books, vols. i and ii; J. Stuart (ed.), *List of pollable persons within the shire of Aberdeen, 1696* (2 vols., Aberdeen 1844). The lists for each parish were largely compiled in September 1695.

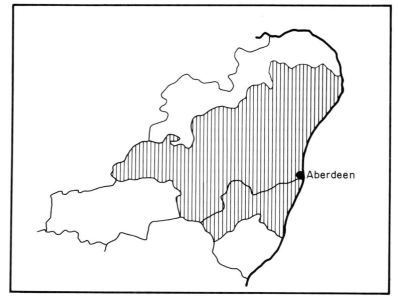

Figure 4. Parishes with knitters, Aberdeenshire and Kincardineshire, 1761. Source: Aberdeen District Archives, Guildry Minute Book, 25 March 1761.

culture surely lies in the composition of the labour force. Although that for cloth was made up mainly of female spinners, the weavers were men and it was they who determined the location of the industry since their labour was more readily available than in areas of predominantly arable farming. By contrast, stockings were made almost entirely by women and their labour was plentiful everywhere, regardless of the type of agriculture practised. Although they might help with peat cutting and the harvest, there were long periods of the year when they were free to knit while the men occupied themselves on the land.

IV

The speed with which the hosiery industry declined was remarkable, though it took a long time for it to disappear completely.

There were two main causes: war with France from 1793 onwards which destroyed overseas markets and, more important in the long run, the rise of the frame-made stocking industry, which in Scotland was centred on Hawick.[29] Some stockings were still made in a number of Aberdeenshire and North Kincardineshire parishes at the time of the *New Statistical Account* (1845), usually those with poor soils and large numbers of small farms and crofts. There were now only nine hosiery merchants in Aberdeen, while in the parish of Birse the organisation of knitting had reverted to its earlier form, with the women providing their own wool. The knitting was done mainly by old women who were fit for nothing else; the average payment for a pair of stockings varied from three pence halfpenny to fivepence and weekly earnings between twelve and eighteenpence. These rates were lower than those in the second part of the eighteenth century, though the latter was for both spinning and knitting whereas in the 1840s the women were required only to knit. Not even these low wages could compete with machine-made stockings, and although some knitters turned to making bonnets and under-jackets for seamen, their days were numbered.[30]

Even before the 1790s the area given over to the knitting of stockings was contracting on two fronts. From South Kincardineshire, the Highland parishes, Strathbogie (which lay in the extreme north-west of Aberdeenshire) and northern Buchan there was a relentless inward expansion of the better paid linen industry though some women preferred knitting since it left them freer to move about. This trend, particularly in Buchan, was associated with the creation between c.1750 and 1840 of planned villages by local landowners who encouraged spinners and weavers to settle there. Eventually their inhabitants specialised in producing linen thread for manufacturers as far away as the East Midlands of England, but competition from factory-produced yarn led to the disappearance of this industry too by the middle of the nineteenth century. There was also the expansion around Aberdeen of a large factory-based industry which relied heavily on water power from the falls on the lower Don (the only major source of water power in the North East) or the streams which flowed into the Dee at its mouth, and on steam-power produced from imported coal. It is estimated that

in 1840 the dozen or so mills in the Aberdeen area gave employment to 12,000 women, though a series of spectacular failures
had reduced this number to 6,000 by the early 1850s.[31]
   The rise of the factory system did not compensate for the
collapse of cottage industries. The peak of full and part-time
employment in textiles was probably reached in 1811, when
George Keith, a man who was not given to exaggeration, put
it at 41,000 or just over 30 per cent of the population of Aberdeenshire.[32] This had been reduced to 8,000, or 3.6 per cent of
the population, by the time of the 1851 census. There is no
way of checking the first figure and that for 1851 may be an
underestimate, but together they provide some indication of a
fall which left rural Aberdeenshire de-industrialised and dependent more than ever upon agriculture, albeit upon an agricultural system that was improving fast. As in most areas with
cottage industries, the industrial revolution meant that far fewer
people were employed in manufacturing.

REFERENCES

1.   The best introduction to proto-industrialisation, which also con-
     tains an excellent bibliography, is L.A. Clarkson, *Proto-indus-
     trialation: the first phase of industrialisation?* (London, 1985).
2.   Duncan Macniven, Merchant and trader in early seventeenth
     century, Aberdeen (Aberdeen University M.Litt.thesis, 1977);
     Duncan Macniven, 'Merchants and traders in early seventeenth
     century Aberdeen' in D. Stevenson (ed.), *From lairds to louns:
     country and burgh life in Aberdeen, 1600-1800* (Aberdeen, 1986), 58-
     91, 64.
3.   T.C. Smout, *Scottish overseas trade on the eve of the Union* (Edinburgh,
     1962), 234-5.
4.   Alexander Skene, *Memorialls for the governments of the royal burghs
     in Scotland* (Aberdeen, 1685), 103-4.
5.   Smout, *Scottish overseas trade*, 234-5.
6.   C Gulvin, *The tweedmakers: a history of the Scottish fancy woollen
     industry 1600-1914* (Newton Abbot, 1973) 21; Skene, *Memorialls*,
     105-6; Smout, *Scottish overseas trade*, 235.
7.   Gulvin, *The tweedmaker*, 32-3; Sir John Sinclair (ed.), *The Stat-*

istical Account of Scotland, 1791-99 [*OSA*] (new ed., Wakefield, 1975-83), xiv 319 (Aberdeen); J. Anderson, *General view of the agriculture* .... *of the county of Aberdeen* (Edinburgh, 1794), 36.

8. I.C.M. Barnes, 'The Aberdeen stocking trade', *Textile History*, viii (1977), 79-99; *SA*, xiv, 319.

9. Macniven, Merchant and Trader (M Litt), 57; Barnes, 'The Aberdeen stocking trade', 83-7; T.Donnelly, 'The Economic activities of the Aberdeen Merchant Guild', *Scottish Economic and Social History Review* (1981), 28; D. Loch, *Essay on the trade, industry and manufacture of Scotland* (Edinburgh, 1775), 23.

10. J. Stuart (ed.), *List of pollable persons within the shire of Aberdeen, 1696* (Aberdeen, 1844), ii, 583-632, The lists for each parish were largely compiled in September 1695.

11. Skene, *Memorialls*, 104; E. Bain, *Merchant and craft guilds: a history of the Aberdeen incorporated trades* (Aberdeen, 1887), 44.

12. Aberdeen District Archives [ADA], Town Council Minutes, i, part I, 105, quoted in Macniven, Merchant and Trader (M.Litt.), 67; ADA, Guildry Minute Book, 1733-93, *passim*.

13. *OSA*, xiv, 318, (Aberdeen); Barnes, 'The Aberdeen stocking trade', *passim*; I.F. Grant, 'An old Scottish handicraft industry', *Scottish Historical Review*, xviii (1921), 282; G.S. Keith, *General view of the agriculture of Aberdeenshire* (Aberdeen 1811), 492-4.

14. *Register of the privy council of Scotland, 1625-7* (1899), 75.

15. R.E. Tyson, 'The population of Aberdeenshire, 1695-1755: a new approach', *Northern Scotland*, vi, no.1 (1985), 125.

16. ADA, Weavers' Enactment Books, i and ii. I am most grateful to Ms Judith Cripps, Aberdeen City Archivist, for drawing my attention to this source.

17. *OSA*, xiv, 320 (Aberdeen).

18. M. Gray, *The Highland economy* (Edinburgh and London, 1957), 20.

19. *OSA*, xv, 7 (Aberdour).

20. *OSA*, xiv and xv, *passim*.

21. *OSA*, xv, 482 (Rayne).

22. F. Douglas, *A general description of the east coast of Scotland* (Aberdeen, 1826), 68.

23. R.E. Tyson, 'Famine in Aberdeenshire, 1695-1699: anatomy of a crisis', in Stevenson (ed.), *From lairds to louns*, 32-52.

24. R. Callander, 'The pattern of landownership in Aberdeenshire in the seventeenth and eighteenth centuries' in Stevenson (ed.), *From lairds to louns*, 5.

25. Skene, *Memorialls*, 102-3.

26. I am grateful to Mr A Gibson (University of Exeter) for providing me with information on this subject; V. Morgan, 'Agri-

cultural wage rates in late eighteenth century Scotland', *Economic History Review*, xxiv, no.2 (1971), 188.

27. *OSA*, xiv, 504 (Glenmuick, Tullich and Glengairn).
28. I. Whyte, 'Agriculture in Aberdeenshire in the seventeenth and eighteenth centuries: continiuity and change' in Stevenson (ed.), *From lairds to louns*, 12; A. Watt, *An early history of Kintore* (Fintray, 1865), 72.
29. Barnes, 'The Aberdeen stocking trades', 91.
30. *New Statistical Account of Scotland*, xii, *Aberdeenshire* (Edinburgh, 1845), *passim*; I.F. Grant, 'An old Scottish handicraft industry', 285-8.
31. R.E. Tyson, 'The economy of Aberdeen', in J.S. Smith and D. Stevenson (eds.), *Aberdeen in the nineteenth century: the making of the modern city* (Aberdeen, 1988), 21.
32. Keith, *General View*, 580-5.

TOOLS AND TILLAGE IN NORTHERN SCOTLAND

Alexander Fenton

Northern Scotland, in which I am including Grampian Region, cannot be considered in isolation from the rest of the country when discussing tools and tillage, for two main reasons. The first is that the influence of Lowland farming penetrated all parts of the north though in differing degrees and in different ways in different places. The second is that the north and west of Scotland long retained what might be described as archaic practices, of kinds that allow us to interpret better the situation in the Lowlands before the full impact of agricultural improvement swept away the bulk of their traces. These two points will be borne in mind in looking at the tools, their techniques of use, and the shape of the farming landscape within which they operated.

It is not my intention to discuss the prehistoric evidence, but to concentrate on the historical period. And since I have published a good deal about implements of tillage, there is no point in repeating detail that is readily available. My purpose today is to look for the broader patterns that tie in with periods of socio-economic change, and at some of the responses to the pressures of such periods.

The inventory of tools for cultivating the soil covers both horse-drawn and hand- and foot-operated equipment. The latter was suited to terrain where the plough could not easily operate, but this is not to say that their areas of use were mutually exclusive. In fact, they had an interesting symbiotic relationship that could extend to techniques of use also.

In Shetland, Orkney, Caithness and on to the Outer

Hebrides, the main type of plough was a single-stilted implement drawn by two or often four animals, oxen or horses (plates 21-2). It is known that timber for ploughs was being imported from Norway to the Northern Isles in 1652. This included plough beams and mould-strokers (attachments fixed where a mould board is placed, but intended not so much to turn over the soil as to break it up, almost as if harrowing). Such single-stilted ploughs had largely died out by the mid-nineteenth century, having been replaced by two-stilted ploughs—examples of which were being brought in by lairds by the mid-eighteenth century—but in Orkney especially some survived alongside south country plough types because of their usefulness in specific tasks like earthing up potatoes. We have here an interesting demonstration of an innovating crop, the potato, introduced to the islands by the 1750s, leading to the continuation of use of an instrument that was otherwise obsolescent.

This was true of Orkney rather than Shetland, where the single-stilted plough became obsolete earlier. This was due to the eighteenth century development of commercial fishing by lairds and merchants, which led to the splitting of earlier, larger farming units (in effect farm 'villages' where much of the seasonal work was done on a cooperative basis) into single farm or croft units that provided a home base for fishermen, though it was their wives and families who had to work them. Economic pressures led in this way to a substantial decline in the use of the single-stilted plough amongst the ordinary folk, and a great increase in the use of the 'dellin' spade', partly by individuals but more by groups of individuals working in teams. It is almost symbolic of the mental attachment of people to ploughing that team-work with the spade could turn over the soil in a manner very reminiscent of elongated plough furrows. In this case, the spade replaced the plough, which is the opposite of what a learned scholar thirled to theories of the rise of man from savagery to civilisation might expect.

I should also draw attention to the fact that there is a good deal of variation amongst Scottish types of single-stilted plough, for example, in the use of mould-strokers or small, double-mouldboards; in the framing of the single handle; but most importantly in the form and nature of the share and coulter.

Fig. 20. Ancient Single Stilted Plough.

Engraved by Chas Thomson, Engr, Edinr

21. A single-stilted Shetland plough drawn by four oxen abreast. S. Hibbert, *A description of the Shetland Islands*, 1822, plate VI, fig. 20. (Scottish Ethnological Archive, National Museums of Scotland [SEA], C1594)

22. An Orkney 'stiltie ploo', drawn by one ox. A man with a pole helps to keep the plough pressed into the ground. (SEA, C1531)

Variety depends on several factors—whether the soil is friable and peaty as often in the Northern Isles, whether it is tough and shallow, as often in the Outer Hebrides, and whether joiners have replaced farmers as the main makers of ploughs. Environmental adaptation is most marked in the case of the Hebridean *crann-nan-gad* with its broad sock and curving coulter, clearly intended to facilitate paring or skimming of the shallow soil, and its down-curved beam whose tip could run on the ground to help in hoisting the plough over an earth-fast stone (plate 23).

There is a major difference between the functioning of single-stilted ploughs, and ordinary two-stilted ploughs. The former did not turn up the soil into a series of ridges and furrows. They worked, therefore, in patches of reasonably well-drained land. But there were many areas in this peat-covered country of ours where the ground was far too soft and boggy for any kind of plough at all. A surrogate had to be used, namely the digging spade with a straight handle and a foot peg or ledge at one side for pressing it into the ground, or the highly specialised *caschrom* with its crooked handle, formed as a lever for undercutting and turning firm turf and for uprooting stones (plate 24). In North West Scotland—but hardly in the Northern Isles, where the spade was often worked in formerly plough-turned ground— the most marked technique was the making of lazy-beds. These are, in effect, raised beds on which crops were grown, with ditches at each side to drain the water (plate 25). They are essentially adaptations of the standard ridge-and-furrow techniques of Lowland ploughing to extreme soil conditions, suited to the working abilities of small social units.

Ridges and furrows were made by the two-stilted plough. The purpose was to create a raised bed with a low furrow alongside by which the surface drainage of the land could be achieved in the days before systematic underground tile drainage, i.e. before the 1830s. Throughout Scotland—except where soil conditions made such drainage less necessary—we can take it that all arable land had a corrugated, ridge-and-furrow appearance. The work was done by the old Scotch plough and by improved plough types developed at the end of the eighteenth century. Each could be found in a number of variations, most of which we must also include in our Northern

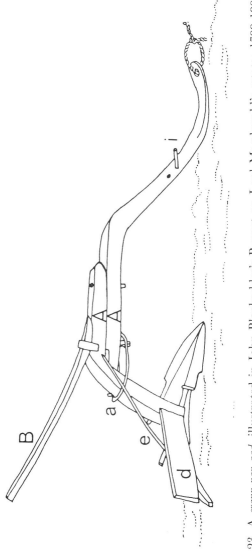

23. A *crann-nan-gad*, illustrated in John Blackadder's Report on Lord Macdonald's estates 1799-1800 (County Record Offices, East Riding of Yorkshire, DDBM/27/3). AA the beam formed of two pieces of wood, joined together by an iron ring, a. B — stilt or handle. d — mould-board, 1 — pin for attachment of yoking, e — pin.

24. Working at lazy-beds with a *caschrom*. A sod is being levered over, after the initial undercutting. (School of Scottish Studies)

25. Lazy-beds in the Uig district of Lewis, some already cultivated. (A. Fenton, 1970s. SEA, 51.57.4)

Scotland inventory. It is this widespread technique of ridging-and-furrowing that must, I think, be seen as a parallel to the lazy bedding of areas of peaty soil and of shallow soil that had to be, so to speak, scraped up into usable beds for oats and barley, and increasingly from the 1740s for potatoes. The conceptual link is further strengthened by the fact that lazy beds were used in the Lowlands about the same period as a means of reclaiming poor land through potato growing; improvements having been made, the plough then took over there.

Reference is commonly made to a strong Highland/Lowland dichotomy marked by differences in terrain and climate, scale of operations, types of tools and equipment, the homes people lived in, the languages they spoke. It is easy to take the superficial view and see these as mutually exclusive. This is not so. I have pointed to the lazy bed and ridge-and-furrow link as an example of an apparently different expression of one and the same concept under differing circumstances. The point becomes even clearer when we consider the plough team and its handling.

The old Scotch plough, in Lowland practice, was pulled by a team of from four to twelve animals, which could be of oxen or sometimes of horses or a mixture of the two, arranged in pairs (plate 26). The average taken for fiscal purposes seems to have been eight oxen, since the unit of land extent called a *ploughgate* was reckoned as the amount eight oxen could work in a year. What a single ox could cope with was an eighth of this, an *oxgate* or *oxgang*. One man stood between the stilts and guided the plough, keeping it tilted to the right angle for working up ridges. Another, usually a laddie, used whip or goad to control and urge on the animals. Because of high man and animal power demands, in the old farming community days fellow tenants had more often than not to club together to make up a full team—and we should not forget that others might follow the plough with spades, breaking clods too big to crumble easily. Thus the immediate old Scotch plough team was of up to twelve animals and two people, with others playing supplementary roles around it.

In the north and west, where land was often worked in patches where the ridge-and-furrow technique was less needed, where horses rather than oxen were the main draught animals,

26. The old Scotch plough, on the end of a table tombstone in Liberton Churchyard, Edinburgh, 1753. There is a team of six: two pairs of oxen and a pair of horses. An assistant urges on the team, and the ploughman holds the stilts only. The field has been ploughed into ridges and furrows. (SEA, XIX. 16.1)

and where altogether lighter plough types, often single-stilted, were in use, the team had a different arrangement. It was smaller, of four to six horses (or sometimes oxen, as in Caithness, Orkney and Shetland) yoked not two by two, but in line abreast. The use of horses in this way was so built into the north and west, as well as Perth, Argyll, Angus and Lanark, that the term *horsegang* replaced *oxgang* or *oxgate* in these areas.

It may seem that here are differences, not similarities, between Highland and Lowland Scotland. But in each case a large team was used, often communally provided, and in each case a helper was used to control the animals. The social system was the same. It was the scale of arable land use, the need for specific ploughing techniques, and the availability of either oxen or horses that led to apparent differences.

It is also possible to point to a basically late eighteenth-nineteenth century phase of continuing pressure from the Lowlands, for there is a particular variety of the old Scotch plough, shorter, lighter and with fairly steeply upturned stilts, called the *crann gaidhealach*, 'Highland plough', by Dwelly in his Gaelic Dictionary. It has been recorded in Aberdeen, Angus, Argyll, Bute, Caithness, the Western Highlands and Islands, Inverness, Kirkcudbright, Orkney, Perth, Stirling, Sutherland,—in short, it was widespread (plate 27). It forms an interface between the two-stilted old Scotch plough and the single-stilted ploughs of the north and west (plates 28a and 28b); that it results from spread and adaptation from core to peripheral areas of the idea of the old Scotch plough is made abundantly clear by the fact that the team used is exactly that for the single-stilted plough— four to six horses abreast, with the ploughman's assistant walking backwards in front of them, urging them on.

By around 1800, therefore, we can see three broad groupings of cultivating implements: the north and west marked by the single-stilted plough, the spade and the caschrom; a diagonal strip from north east to south west Scotland broadly based on the highland line marked by the light form of the old Scotch plough and the Highland form of team, and the arable Lowland areas marked by the old Scotch plough and by the improved two-horse plough which eventually spread throughout Scotland.

I want to return to spades for a moment, to introduce an

27. A lightened version of the old Scotch plough, drawn by two pairs of horses yoked two by two. A helper controls the team and the ploughman sees to the plough. (W. Aberdeen, Plan of Castlehill, Caithness, 1772. Scottish Record Office, RHP 1220. SEA, C2548)

essential aspect of tillage, the need to provide fertiliser. Leaving aside the droppings of stock and the use of seaweed at the coasts, the major resource available was the peat and turf with which northern Scotland abounded to an even greater degree than in the south. It was worth much. Peat itself was an almost ubiquitous fuel, cut in the mosses and burned in the floor-level hearths. The ashes went out to the byres to help to soak up the urine and to return to the fields with the rest of the muck (plate 29). A variety of peat-spade types, adapted to the quality and type of peat, is known throughout Scotland, and much peat is still being cut for fuel. Turf, cut with a *flauchter spade* or flaying spade, was sometimes burned also if peat as such had began to wear out near a settlement. It had a great range of other uses: as a material for building fold dykes and the walls of buildings, as roofing material, as an element in the ubiquitous earthen middens or 'yirdie tams' that could be composted with byre manure and kitchen refuse, and so on. In any or all of these uses, it was likely to find its way back to the fields to enrich them, returning the energy to the source from which it came. Though lime had become recognised as a fertiliser—and this included the burning of sea shells—from the seventeenth century, it took a long time for it to begin to replace or supplement systems of turf-based manuring that had some degree of antiquity and were known in other countries besides.

A special way of treating peaty ground deserves mention. I am not speaking of *muirburn*, carried out already by the sixteenth century to improve grazing, but of the practice of burning bogs to fit them for arable use. The 'Description of Aberdeen and Banff' of 1662 spoke of burning the mosses, to make them fertile and fit for the plough. The burning process was repeated after a couple of years, and 'crops luxuriate wonderfully with the ashes'. Another source for Buchan, probably also of the seventeenth century, tells how sods were cast from one piece of ground and then carted to another where they were burned as a fertiliser. There is evidence of a third method, also from Aberdeenshire, recorded in 1735. This involved using the plough to make ridges of peaty soil, the highest furrows of which were gathered into heaps and burned; or the ground could be ribbed with small furrows, the upcast of which was gathered and burned; or the field could be ploughed, left for a time, then burned in spring, before sowing, by using heaps of combustible turf to get it going. Perhaps this last one is what the Description referred to. Without going into more detail, we can say that the practice of using burned turf as a fertiliser—commemorated in the common place-name, Bruntlands—was well-developed in seventeenth and eighteenth century Grampian. The practice was also known in Kincardineshire (1735), in Lanarkshire (1790s), Nairn, Moray, Dumbarton and Galloway (all eighteenth century). The tradition was strong. Much land must have been reclaimed for arable use by this method; and though that practice had more or less died out by about 1800, it is worth remembering that fertilisation by burning is or was widespread

28(a)

28(b)

28. A lightened version of the old Scotch plough, showing (a) the wooden mould-board and the open-work sock; (b) the land-side, with the four-sided frame formed by the junction of beam, sheath, left-hand stilt, and sole. (A. Fenton, 1970s. SEA, II.44.6)

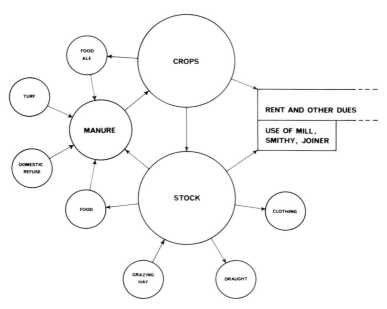

29. A model for the pre-improvement farming community, showing the prominent place of manure, and the self-supporting nature of the enterprise. Only rent, dues, and a small number of essential food and work related costs went out of the community. (SEA, C18661)

in the world, particularly in relation to the clearing of woodland patches. We seem to be looking at traces in Grampian of part of the last elements of the long, slow spread of the pattern of human settlement just before the coming of the full impact of the Agricultural Revolution.

The point is reinforced further by the same 1662 Description. In considering former farming village settlements on units of land called *daachs* or *davochs*, said by the writer to equate with as much land as could be tilled by four ploughs, he wrote that though in the higher districts the boundaries of the *daachs* could still be seen, the homestead units were no longer in nucleated groups. The woods around having been cut down, four ploughs were no longer enough to handle the arable area. The proprietors of the land then divided it up, so that the homesteads 'were continuous but not nucleated'. The farm villages were abandoned and the farmers moved each to his own possession or whatever fertile soil attracted him. Gordon remembered this procedure from his young days, the early 1600s.

This is a very important comment in terms of our farming landscape. It reinforces the role of lairds in changing farming practices in relation to associated forms of settlement. It demonstrates the existence of farming villages at this period, of the kind, no doubt, that are still perfectly familiar in Middle Europe. And it points forward to coming new days in Scottish farming, to the individualisation of farm units where each farm stood in its own fields, separated by walls, dykes or fences from its neighbours, in a way that visitors from other European lands find worthy of remark.

Traces of the older farm village system have remained till today, however. The township of Auchindrain in Argyll is an example, and others are to be found in Shetland. But even in the crofting counties where farm villages lasted longest, much imposed change went on. Nucleated settlements in the straths were moved to the coasts or to the edges of peat bogs. They left the way clear for sheep farms, and resited the manpower to suit commercial needs like fishing and kelp-burning, or farming needs like reclamation around the edges of bigger farms. The layout of the fields was ladder-like or radial, but the individualising principle of one croft per unit of land within the township complex was followed. There was one difference from the Lowlands, however. Though the crofts stood on their own arable fields, outside the hill dykes the grazing of sheep was still done in common. In this, a vestige of the old communal farm villages remains.

It is not possible to make general statements about farming changes in northern Scotland, partly because of the variety of environments and partly because of the effects of socio-economic pressures applied by the people above. I mentioned at the beginning how fishing needs depressed farming in Shetland. That is one extreme. At the opposite end of the scale is Easter Ross, which deserves close study for the way it came to fall into the high farming pattern of the southern counties of Scotland during the late eighteenth and nineteenth centuries. The process can be seen from the survey of the estate of Cadboll by George Brown in 1813. Many farms then had patches of 'new land', mixed with arable and grazing in large numbers of patches, much of it described as wet, boggy, covered with bushes, moor with some whins, alder wood, broom. Commons still existed, providing turf and poor pasture. There were some multiple crofts in the parish of Rosskeen. The farm of Ballnaskerrish in the parish of Tarbet was possessed by two tenants 'in Runridge'. The old days were still showing their traces. But the survey shows also how the older farms were being rearranged, and large numbers of patches of arable and pasture blocked out into units. Allied to this activity was a strong East Lothian link. In 1798, George Mackenzie from East Lothian took Meikle Tarrel on a nineteen year lease; the farm was increased to 250-260 acres arable, on land previously held by several tenants. He brought with him his own south country servants, horses and implements. He had specialist ploughmen for his five pairs of horse, and worked the land in four shifts, each containing four breaks of sixty acres. He bought and fattened four year old stots for the south market, and had a herd of pigs whose mature carcases were shipped south from Portmahomack. Archibald Dudgeon, also from East Lothian, entered Arboll in 1802, again bringing his own implements, horses and servants. He grew large acreages of turnips to fatten Cheviot wedders for the south market. Local farmers also succumbed, for MacLeod of Geanies engaged an East Lothian grieve to help with promulgating his improvements. It is hardly necessary to emphasise farther how Easter Ross became a highly advanced farming area able to compete with any part of Scotland.

The ground I have covered has had a limited intention: to look primarily at pre-improved conditions and survivals, to touch on clues that point to the final stages of a long spreading of the settlement pattern in the days before the onset of the agricultural improvement period, and to consider aspects of the range of inter-relationships between the North and South of Scotland. I am very aware of the amount of work still to be done on the subject. Let this serve, however, as what the Germans call a *Vorspeise*, and the English, following the French, an *hors d'oeuvres*.

SOURCES

The above paper is based on the following sources, which may be consulted for further details and illustrations.

A. Fenton, 'Early and traditional cultivating implements in Scotland', *Proceedings of the Society of Antiquaries of Scotland*, xcvi (1962-3), 264-317.

A. Fenton, 'The Chilcarroch Plough', *Scottish Studies*, viii (1964), 80-4.

A. Fenton, 'A plough type from the Outer Isles of Scotland', *Tools and Tillage*, i, no.2 (1969), 117-28.

A. Fenton, 'Paring and burning and the cutting of turf and peat in Scotland', A. Gailey and A. Fenton (eds.), *The spade in Northern and Atlantic Europe* (Ulster Folk Museum, 1970), 155-93.

A. Fenton, 'The cas-chrom. A review of the Scottish evidence', in *Tools and Tillage*, ii, no.3 (1974), 131-49.

A. Fenton, *Scottish country life* (Edinburgh, 1976), chapter 2.

A. Fenton, *The Northern Isles: Orkney and Shetland* (Edinburgh, 1978).

A. Fenton, 'Seawood manure, paring and burning. The cutting of turf and peat', in *The shape of the past* (Edinburgh, 1986), vol.ii, parts II and III.

A. Fenton, *Country life in Scotland. Our rural past* (Edinburgh, 1987), chapters 1-3, 11.

Robert Gordon of Straloch, 'Notes for a description of the two shires of Aberdeen and Banff', W. Macfarlane, *Geographical Collections*, ed. A. Mitchell, ii (Scottish History Society, 1907), 224-306. First published in 1662 in the second edition of Blaen's *Atlas*.

The information for easter Ross is from the contents and estimate of the estate of Cadboll belonging to Robert Bruce Agneas McLeod Esquire, from a survey taken by Geo. Brown 1813, containing the parishes of Rosskeen, Kilmuir and Tarbet, a manuscript kindly lent by Mrs Jane Durham.